MURDER & MAYHEM

—— IN ——

NORTHEAST OKLAHOMA

LARRY WOOD

THE
History
PRESS

Published by The History Press
Charleston, SC
www.historypress.com

First published 2024

Manufactured in the United States

ISBN 9781467156820

Library of Congress Control Number: 2024941841

CONTENTS

PREFACE

As a freelance writer from Joplin, Missouri, who specializes in local and regional history, particularly the Civil War and true crime, I have written about many notorious incidents in southwest Missouri. I've also written extensively about infamous events in southeast Kansas. In fact, two of my previous books for The History Press are *Murder and Mayhem in Missouri* and *Murder and Mayhem in Southeast Kansas*. Since I live only three or four miles from the Oklahoma state line, I decided it was time to tackle northeast Oklahoma as well.

During the 1800s and very early 1900s, most of northeast Oklahoma was part of Indian Territory, while a small portion of it was part of Oklahoma Territory. In either case, the region was mostly occupied and governed by Natives, who, in general, were not eager to cooperate with United States government officials. Thus, the region became a haven for fugitives from U.S. law. The Cookson Hills, in particular, earned a reputation as an outlaw hideout, a reputation that continued into the gangster era of the Depression years and beyond. Suffice it to say that northeast Oklahoma has harbored more than its share of desperadoes and witnessed more than its share of notorious incidents.

This book details fifteen of those episodes in roughly chronological order from before the Civil War until modern times. Most of the incidents, like the Tulsa Race Massacre, are well known, while a few of them are relatively obscure. I find that the obscure events are often more interesting to research and write about than the incidents a lot of people are already familiar with.

The discerning reader will notice that the incidents I've chosen to include in the book are tilted toward the early years of the chronology. This is by design, as I enjoy researching and writing about the old stuff more than I enjoy writing about recent events. Anything that I can remember hearing about when it was news seems less like history to me than events that I have no personal recollection of—and my memory stretches back at least fifty years. However, I have included a couple of incidents from the past half-century, not only to lend the book a measure of balance but also because the two events I've chosen were notorious and sensational enough that they almost demanded inclusion.

For the purposes of this book, I have defined northeast Oklahoma as the northeast quadrant of the main part of the state (in other words, the northeast quadrant after the panhandle is lopped off). By this definition, Tulsa and the surrounding areas are included in the book, while Oklahoma City is not.

ACKNOWLEDGEMENTS

I did most of the research for this book online, so I had few face-to-face interactions with live human beings. However, I do want to mention a few people who were especially helpful as I gathered information and illustrations: Jon May of the Oklahoma Historical Society, Melissa Weiss of the Western History Collections of the University of Oklahoma Libraries, and Angie Rush of the Three Rivers Museum.

I want to thank my wife, Gigi, not only for reading parts of the manuscript and offering suggestions but also for her unwavering support of my writing efforts.

I appreciate the encouragement and advice of acquisitions editor Ben Gibson as I prepared the manuscript for submission. I also want to thank copy editor Ashley Hill for her thorough edit of the manuscript. Her attention to detail has made the book a better, more polished product.

THE MURDER OF ELIAS BOUDINOT AND THE RIDGES

More than any other major Native tribe, the Cherokee used diplomacy and legal arguments during the late 1700s and early 1800s to protect their interests. They negotiated a series of treaties with the U.S. government that ceded certain tribal lands while protecting other ancestral lands in the Southeast. However, white settlers kept pouring into the tribe's lands with the tacit approval of the federal government and often with the open approval of state governments. Angry and frustrated by the flood of white settlers and the failure of the federal government to uphold the treaties, Major Ridge and other tribal leaders met in council in October 1829 and adopted a resolution calling for any member of the tribe who signed further treaties ceding Cherokee lands to be subject to the death penalty. Ridge likely never considered that he might one day suffer the very penalty that he himself had prescribed.[1]

The encroachment of white settlers on Cherokee land continued into the 1830s, however. State governments looked the other way and even passed laws to protect the white settlers. The U.S. government, meanwhile, declined to enforce the provisions of treaties previously signed with the Cherokee that protected the tribe's lands. President Andrew Jackson, who viewed all Natives as savages, pressured the tribe to cede their lands in exchange for lands west of the Mississippi River.[2]

Major Ridge and Cherokee tribal chief John Ross, once strong allies, gradually split over the issue of Native removal. Major Ridge, perhaps influenced by his son John Ridge, took an increasingly pragmatic view. The

younger Ridge had received a classic American-European education in Connecticut and was married to a white woman. He and his father came to believe that the best way to maintain the tribe's autonomy and protect its interests was to accept Native removal to the West, while Ross refused to entertain such a proposal.[3]

In late 1835, the Ridges and other leaders of the pro-removal faction signed a treaty with the federal government at New Echota (Georgia), agreeing to cede Cherokee lands in the Southeast in exchange for cash and designated lands in present-day Oklahoma. This was done while John Ross was in Washington, D.C., and without the approval of the majority of the tribe. Apparently aware of the previous "blood oath" he had supported, Major Ridge was reported to have said after signing the treaty that he had just signed his own death warrant.[4]

A deep schism developed in the tribe between the minority who favored the treaty as the most practical course and the large majority who adamantly opposed it. The Ridge faction came to be known as the Treaty Party, while opponents were called the Anti-Treaty Party. Although they identified as Cherokee, most of the Treaty Party members were mixed-race individuals who had intermarried with white settlers and adopted the American-European culture. Most of the Anti-Treaty Party, on the other hand, were full-blood Cherokees who clung to old tribal customs. A notable exception was John Ross, the chief of the tribe and leader of the Anti-Treaty Party, who was only one-eighth Cherokee by blood.[5]

The Anti-Treaty Party sent a petition to Washington, D.C., signed by 3,352 Cherokee, that urged for the New Echota Treaty to be rejected on the

Opposite, left: Lithograph of Major Ridge. *Library of Congress.*

Opposite, right: Lithograph of John Ross. *Library of Congress.*

Left: Lithograph of John Ridge. *Library of Congress.*

grounds that Chief Ross did not sign it and those who did sign it were not authorized to do so. Despite the objection, the treaty was narrowly ratified by Congress in the spring of 1836 and signed into law by President Jackson.[6]

The Treaty Party, composed of about two thousand Cherokees, moved to Indian Territory (present-day Oklahoma) in 1837. They were provided transportation by the government and treated well because of their cooperation. Ross and the other members of the Anti-Treaty Party refused to make the trek, however, until they were rounded up and forced to do so in the fall of 1838. As many as four thousand men, women, and children of the sixteen thousand who started the trip died during the ensuing journey, which came to be known as the Trail of Tears. The suffering and hardship they endured further embittered the Anti-Treaty Party against the Treaty Party, who had preceded them in the trip to Oklahoma.[7]

After the Anti-Treaty Party arrived in their new land, they called a meeting to try to effect a union among themselves, the Treaty Party, and the Old Settlers (or the Cherokees who had come west years earlier) and adopt a consensus government. Held in June 1839 at Double Springs, about four miles northwest of Tahlequah, the meeting ended in an impasse. The Old Settlers had established a government years earlier, but they were not hostile to terms outlined by the new arrivals, the majority of whom were members of the Anti-Treaty Party. However, Ridge and his associates insisted on maintaining the previously established government and officers as a condition of any union.[8]

After the meeting at Double Springs broke up on June 21, about three hundred Anti-Treaty Party members met in secret later the same day and invoked the old "blood" law that Major Ridge himself had once espoused. A small percentage of those present were appointed to be the executioners after they drew lots out of a hat.[9]

The next day, June 22, near daylight, a mob of about forty men came to the home of John Ridge on Honey Creek in the northeast part of Indian Territory near present-day Southwest City, Missouri. They entered the home undetected and burst a cap at his head as he slept beside his wife. Startled from his sleep by the misfire, Ridge awoke and, seeing his impending fate, begged for mercy. He entreated the mob to hear him out, to which one member of the death squad reportedly cried out, "You would not hear us! We asked for mercy, and you turned away and even denied we had spoken."[10]

After the gun malfunctioned, the mob took Ridge from his bed, dragged him outside into the yard, and "butchered him in a most savage, brutal manner by stabbing him in the body some twenty-seven times." They then threw him into the air as high as they could, and when the dying man landed on the ground, "Each one stamped upon the body as they marched over it by single file, until the last man of them had performed his fiendish purpose."[11]

This "tragedy" was enacted in front of Ridge's wife and children, and "the shock to Mrs. Ridge was more than she could bear," as "she was seized with spasms, which [threatened] her life."[12]

After killing John Ridge, the executioners went in pursuit of his father, Major Ridge. He had left his home for Arkansas the day before, but the mob overtook him on the evening of June 22 near the Arkansas state line and shot him dead from his horse.[13]

The same day, June 22, Elias Boudinot, the nephew of Major Ridge, was working on his home at Park Hill, a Cherokee settlement near Tahlequah, where Chief John Ross's home was also located. Boudinot, a prominent Treaty Party leader like his uncle, left with three other men to go to a nearby doctor's home to obtain medicine. When they were about halfway to the doctor's house, Boudinot's three companions, secret members of the death squad, suddenly turned on him and killed him.[14]

In the aftermath of the slaughter, John Ross was accused of authorizing it, but the best evidence seems to suggest that the killings were carried out in secret without the tribal chief's knowledge. Stand Watie, who was Boudinot's brother, and other Treaty Party members swore revenge, and federal troops were summoned from Fort Gibson to help keep the peace for a brief time. They were quickly dismissed, and a tentative truce was fashioned between the warring factions.[15]

Elias Boudinot portrait.
Library of Congress.

Editorial comments about the Ridge and Boudinot murders were about as divided as the warring factions of the Cherokee tribe themselves. For instance, a correspondent from Newton County, Missouri, in a St. Louis newspaper, called the killings "a bloody tragedy…which for brutality, almost beggars description." The writer seemed to clearly sympathize with the Ridge family in his description of John Ridge's murder. On the other hand, a letter writer from Indian Territory, shortly after the murders, suggested that the Ridge party brought the killings on themselves by insisting on maintaining the minority government that had been established prior to the arrival of the Anti-Treaty Party. "Had Ridge and his friends retired quietly into private life, and no more interfered to disturb the peace of the nation," the correspondent said, "they would no doubt have lived." Instead, the Ridges had "sealed their own fate" by "rousing the latent indignation of the populace," knowing well that, based on the law drawn up by John Ridge himself, they could be put to death.[16]

Several initial reports of the Ridge killings published in East Coast newspapers suggested that as many as thirty or forty Treaty Party members had been slain during the Anti-Treaty Party's vendetta. But the three leaders were the only ones killed, at least during the initial bloodbath.

However, despite the fragile truce fashioned in the immediate wake of the Ridge killings, acts of violence between the two sides continued to sporadically break out over the next twenty years, and the old resentments carried over even into the Civil War years and beyond. Former members of the Treaty Party tended to side with the Confederacy, whereas most Anti-Treaty Party members sided with the Union. And both sides used the cover of war to discharge old grudges. Confederate general Stand Watie and troops under his command, for instance, are reported to have burned the John Ross home during the war.[17]

2
THE GOINGSNAKE GUNFIGHT

"There are always two sides to every story" is an adage that is often cited to explain the fact that accounts of the same event can vary widely, depending on the perspective and bias of the person telling the story. Perhaps there is no better illustration of that adage than the conflicting accounts of the Goingsnake Tragedy that left eleven people dead and another ten injured near Christie in present-day Adair County, Oklahoma, on April 15, 1872.

The two sides, in this case, were the U.S. Marshals Service and the Cherokee Nation. Ezekial "Zeke" Proctor, a Cherokee Native, had killed Polly Beck, a Cherokee woman, and wounded her white husband, J.L. Kesterson, on February 13 at the Hildebrand Mill, near present-day Colcord, Oklahoma. Because both Proctor and Beck were Cherokee, the Cherokee Nation had jurisdiction in the murder case, and Proctor was scheduled for trial on April 15 at the Goingsnake District Court near Christie. Kesterson was also considered Cherokee under the law because he was married to a Cherokee woman, but shortly before the murder trial was set to begin, Kesterson traveled to Fort Smith, renounced his Cherokee citizenship, and filed a complaint of assault in U.S. court against Proctor. The U.S. Marshals Service then claimed jurisdiction in the assault case, but the Cherokee Nation considered Kesterson an adopted citizen and resented any interference in the matter by the U.S. government.[18]

In addition to the jurisdictional dispute, a volatile mixture of personal grudges and internecine resentments dating to the Cherokee tribe's removal to Oklahoma from their ancestral homelands in the Southeast

Ezekial "Zeke" Proctor. *Oklahoma Historical Society.*

in the late 1830s also contributed to the highly charged atmosphere surrounding the Proctor case.

Both Zeke Proctor and Polly Beck had white blood, but Proctor was a member of the Keetoowah Society, a Cherokee group that wanted to preserve traditional tribal customs and maintain tribal purity as much as possible. Proctor's family had aligned with the Anti-Treaty Party, which was composed largely of full-blooded Cherokees, at the time of the tribe's removal from the Southeast, and Proctor had fought for the Union during the Civil War. Beck's family, on the other hand, had sided with the mixed-blood Treaty Party, and her relatives had fought for the Confederacy during the war.[19]

As if that weren't enough, Proctor was also entangled in a family feud with Kesterson and his Cherokee wife. Kesterson had previously been married to Proctor's sister, but Kesterson had deserted her and her children and started working for Polly Beck Hildebrand at the Hildebrand Mill, which she'd inherited from her previous husband, Stephen Hildebrand. She married Kesterson in March 1871, a marriage that angered Proctor. Not only did Proctor oppose interracial marriage between Cherokee women and white men on moral and political grounds, but he was also especially infuriated by Polly's latest marriage because of Kesterson's abandonment of his sister. To add one more bubble to Proctor's cauldron of resentments, Polly was said to be an attractive woman, and according to at least one report, Proctor might have had a romantic interest in her at one time.[20]

At any rate, Proctor traveled to the mill on February 13, reportedly to settle a dispute over some livestock. He found J.L. Kesterson and Polly Beck there alone. What happened next is just one of several questions on which the two sides of this tragic story disagree. Kesterson told authorities in Fort Smith that Proctor immediately walked up to Polly and shot her dead without provocation before turning the gun on Kesterson and firing shots at him. Proctor, on the other hand, claimed the shooting of Polly Beck was an accident. According to this account, Proctor and Kesterson argued and Proctor started to shoot at Kesterson, but Polly jumped between the two men to protect her husband just as the weapon was fired.[21]

Proctor turned himself in to the Goingsnake District sheriff, Jack Wright. However, Polly's relatives, furious over her killing, felt Proctor would never be convicted in a Cherokee court, and they wanted him tried in the U.S. court at Fort Smith for the attempted murder of a white man. Encouraged by Polly's cousin White Sut Beck, Kesterson went to Fort Smith on April 11, four days before Proctor's trial was set to begin in the Goingsnake District, and filed charges against Proctor.[22]

On April 13, a posse of seven men headed by Deputy U.S. Marshals Jacob F. Owens and Joseph G. Peavey left Fort Smith with instructions to attend the trial of Proctor and to arrest him for the assault on Kesterson if he was not convicted of the Beck murder. Along the way, the posse was joined by a few other men, including White Sut Beck and other Beck clan members, making a total of eleven men.[23]

Proctor's trial had been switched from the regular Goingsnake District Courthouse to the nearby Whitmire Schoolhouse because that building was considered safer and easier to protect. The trial had just gotten underway late in the morning of April 15 when the posse of U.S. marshals and deputies arrived. What happened next, like nearly everything else in the Proctor case, is not clear. About the only consensus is that all hell broke loose, and when the shooting finally stopped, nine men lay dead, two were mortally wounded, and several others were seriously injured.[24]

According to an account provided by one of the deputy marshals a day or two after the bloody shootout and spelled out in a Fort Smith newspaper on April 22, the posse dismounted about fifty yards from the schoolhouse, tied their horses, and filed toward the east side of the building in twos. The posse paused at the corner of the building, and White Sut Beck stepped around to the front door to look in. When he saw a large number of armed men inside, he turned to leave, but "not before he was fired upon and dangerously wounded in the act of turning."[25]

At the same time, a volley of fire poured from the schoolhouse toward the marshals outside. The deputies began to return fire but "were at a great disadvantage, as the attacking force was under shelter, inside the Court House."[26]

White Sut Beck had some friends inside the courthouse, and when they saw him fall, they opened fire inside the building on his enemies. "Presently the fighting was general and fierce inside and outside the Court House. It was brief…but terrible in its results."[27]

The deputy who filed the report in the wake of the gunfight counted seven of the eleven men from the marshal force lying dead, while only three of the Proctor party were killed. Sixteen or seventeen men were wounded, including Deputy Marshal Owens, who was mortally wounded.[28]

THE CHEROKEE MASSACRE.

Full and Thrilling Details of the Affair.

Thirteen Dead and Twelve Wounded—Robbing the Dead—Attempt of the Indians to Murder the Federal Wounded Within the State.

"Thrilling details" of the Goingsnake massacre. *From the* Chicago Evening Mail.

The Fort Smith newspaper referred to Proctor as a "woman killer and desperado" who was "said to have…committed eighteen murders." The editor suggested that the Proctor party was lying in wait for the deputies and ambushed them without provocation. He blamed the tragedy on the "distrust and jealousy" with which many inhabitants of Indian Territory, misled by "bad white men," regarded U.S. officials. Consequently, these unenlightened inhabitants bore "a deadly resentment" against any interference on the part of the U.S. government.[29]

The Cherokee side of the story was entirely different. About two hours after the bloody gunfight ended, William Penn Boudinot, the editor of the *Tahlequah Cherokee Advocate*, arrived on the scene and recorded what he saw:

> *What a sight met our gaze when we rode up to the small school-house where the Court had been called. Three men were lying just before the doorstep in those negligent and still postures so terrifying to the living. Dark pools of blood issuing from each told the horrible story of the manner of their death. In the house lying side by side, with their hats over their faces, lay three more bodies.…A few steps off the deputies right of the door lay the body of a man with light hair and blue eyes, which betokened his white extraction. Next to the chimney behind the house was another, and near by partly supported against the wall was a man groaning in the anguish of a desperate wound. In the bushes a little further off was another corpse of a youth who had staggered there to die. Looking at the living we saw the Presiding Judge, B.H. Sixkiller, with his wrist bandaged, where he had been seriously wounded by two bullets. The prisoner [i.e., Proctor] was limping about with a bullet in the bone of his leg below the knee. Others were wounded more or less. At the nearest residence was lying desperately wounded Deputy Marshal Owens, a man generally respected on both sides of the "line." Some of the badly wounded we did not see, they having fled or been taken care of by their friends. The spectacle which harrowed our sight was the most awful without any comparison that we have ever witnessed.*

After talking to witnesses, Boudinot also offered an account from a Cherokee perspective of what had happened prior to his arrival: "A company of whites, headed by a Cherokee [i.e. White Sut Beck] appeared on the court ground, and without any premonition or intimation of their business, commenced firing into the court-room."

White Sut walked up to the sheriff just inside the door of the schoolhouse and told him to stand out of the way. When Sheriff Wright complied,

White Sut said to Proctor, who was just behind the sheriff, "You damned coward." He then shoved a double-barrel shotgun toward the prisoner. Proctor grabbed the barrel of the gun and pulled it down between his legs as it discharged, with only one ball entering his leg. Then all hell broke loose. The fact that Proctor and his attorney were the first targets of the assault, Boudinot opined, "displayed the object of the murderous attack."

Boudinot praised the guards, whose duty it was to hold and protect the prisoner. Consisting of only four or five men, the group "responded with a degree of unshaken resolution and courage which has rarely been paralleled in history. The attacking party was finally beaten off, and ran off leaving their horses and some of their weapons behind them, and not a few comparatively of their number dead on the scene of their lawless attack."

Boudinot did not learn until after he'd been at the scene some time that the attacking party was a posse of the U.S. Marshals Service whose purpose was to arrest Proctor if he was acquitted. The editor faulted the posse members for not identifying themselves or announcing their purpose when they first arrived on the scene. He said none of the white men in the posse spoke at all and that "the Cherokees accompanying only opened their lips to order the Sheriff and others to clear the way." Boudinot concluded that "the shooting was commenced by the assailants without notice or command, and was, in short, totally unprovoked and with 'malice aforethought.'"

He explained that no movement whatsoever was made to oppose the posse members up until the time that they started shooting. The Cherokee authorities had been left totally in the dark and were left to draw their conclusion based entirely on the actions of the posse. Those actions left no doubt that "mischief of the most murderous sort was meant, unjustified by even the flimsiest pretext of authority."

"What could a conscientious guard do but resist?" the editor asked rhetorically. He then reiterated that the actions of the guard in resisting the posse were "not only right and lawful but heroic."

The whole tragic incident could have been avoided, Boudinot editorialized, if the Cherokees had not forfeited the right of jurisdiction in all matters concerning adopted citizens. They had carelessly surrendered that right during treaty negotiations with the U.S. government because they thought it was an insignificant question. But Boudinot proclaimed that without that right, "Our privilege of self-government is a farce."[30]

Sheriff Wright's report to the principal chief of the Cherokee Nation, written the day after the gunfight, echoed Boudinot's observations from the day before. Wright said that a party of about ten men came riding up, dismounted, and cocked their guns as they marched toward the courthouse. White Sut Beck, with a double-barrel shotgun in his hands, ordered the sheriff to stand aside, and "a moment later one of the same party fired into the house at someone, said to be the prisoner."

White Sut Beck, who had been the person most active in trying to get Proctor prosecuted, led the deputy marshals' party. And that party's "hostile demonstrations against the prisoner" prompted the guard to resist, which, according to the sheriff, was reasonable and right for them to do.

"Even if it were right for the deputy marshals to forcibly seize a prisoner from under charge of a Cherokee guard," said Wright, "and that during the holding of court for his trial, I cannot but think that a violent assault of the kind described, without previous warning, information or demand whatever, is totally indefensible and unjustifiable."

Sheriff Wright added that Deputy Marshal Owens, while lying wounded, had declared that the attacking party acted against his wishes, that he tried in vain to stop them, and that their actions were against his direct orders.[31]

Although the Cherokee side of this tragic story, as provided in the immediate wake of the event, was arguably more convincing in its detail than the U.S. marshals' side, it was the marshals' side that was largely adopted by the white press and propagated throughout the country. Even the term by which the incident is known was largely fixed by the initial report in the Fort Smith newspaper, which claimed the deputy marshals had been massacred. The shootout did, indeed, come to be known as the Goingsnake Massacre. Only in recent years has the term "Goingsnake Tragedy" been put forward as a more objective name for the deadly gunfight that took place in Adair County over 150 years ago.

3

NED CHRISTIE

HERO OR VILLAIN?

Much like Zeke Proctor, Ned Christie was viewed in an entirely different light by much of the Cherokee Nation from the way he was portrayed in the American press. To newspapermen across the country, Christie was a notorious desperado who'd killed a deputy U.S. marshal in an ambush. But many Cherokees thought he was wrongly accused of murder by a repressive federal government, and his resistance to arrest was nothing short of heroic.

As is often the case when opinions differ so greatly, the truth probably lies somewhere in between those extremes. Although there is no evidence to suggest that Christie was a heartless killer, as he was often portrayed in contemporaneous newspapers, to say that he was a "good, peaceable citizen," as at least one Cherokee observer remarked after he became a suspect in the deputy marshal's death, is a bit of a stretch as well.[32]

The son of Watt Christie, Ned (known by Cherokees as Nede Wade) was born in December 1852 in Indian Territory. He was a member of the Keewootah Society, an organization that sought to preserve traditional Cherokee culture and maintain the tribe's sovereignty, and in the fall of 1885, he was elected to the Executive Council of the Cherokee Nation.[33]

A look at Christie's life prior to the election, however, suggests that he was not what one might normally think of as a temperate, peace-loving citizen. Christie had already gone through three wives, two of whom had divorced him, by the beginning of 1885, and several of his family members had been involved in violent incidents. Then in January

1885, Christie shot and killed William Palone while the two were hunting together, reportedly because Christie took it as an insult to his mother when Palone called him a "son of a bitch."[34]

Charged with manslaughter, Christie was acquitted later in 1885, when others who'd been at the scene of the shooting testified that they had not seen who shot Palone. Christie's election to the executive council came still later that same year, so his shooting of Palone must have done little, if anything, to taint his reputation among Cherokee citizens.[35]

A year and a half later, Christie was still serving on the council, and around May 1, 1887, he traveled from his home on Barren Fork in the Goingsnake District to the Cherokee capital at Tahlequah, about twelve miles to the west, for a session of the council. On the evening of May 4, Deputy U.S. Marshal Daniel Maples, who was on his way to Fort Gibson, camped at Hendricks Spring at the north edge of Tahlequah. He and a traveling companion went into town to purchase supplies and started back to camp. As they were getting ready to step onto a footbridge to cross a stream to reach their camp, Maples's companion spotted a gunman lurking in the shadows of a tree on the other side. The man had a pistol pointed in their direction. The companion yelled out, "Don't shoot!" But the assassin fired anyway. The ball struck Maples in the right breast and tore through his body. Both he and his companion managed to return fire, but the shooter escaped into the darkness. The deputy marshal was taken to a local doctor, but he died the next day.[36]

Suspicion for the murder quickly fell on Ned Christie and several other Cherokee Natives who had been seen in the vicinity of where the shooting had taken place and who had previously been in trouble with the law or were known to oppose the U.S. marshals' authority in the Cherokee Nation. In late July 1887, a grand jury indicted Christie and three other men: John Parris, Charley Bobtail, and Bud Trainer. After Trainer's arrest, he fingered Christie as the trigger man in the murder of Maples and claimed Christie did not deny his guilt. The three other indicted men posted bond and were released, but Christie decided to go on the lam rather than put his fate in the hands of a federal court, especially the one at Fort Smith, where Isaac Parker, the so-called hanging judge, had jurisdiction. Contrary to Trainer's allegation, Christie insisted that he was innocent, but he wanted to be tried by a jury of his peers in a tribal court.[37]

Thus began what came to be called "Ned Christie's War," his years-long resistance to arrest by deputy U.S. marshals. With friends and family serving as lookouts or harboring him, Christie frustrated the federal lawmen by eluding capture. As one newspaper commentator said in late December 1887, shortly after the three other suspects in the Maples murder had been taken into custody, Christie was "still at large and remains around Tahlequah, right under the nose of the authorities in that nation, who never molest him. Of course, he takes to the woods when a deputy marshal is known to be in the neighborhood."[38]

In early 1888, a report circulated that Christie had killed a fellow Cherokee named Bear Grinnett. A dispatch from Fort Smith at the time said Christie was a "noted desperado and supposed slayer of Deputy Dan Maples." Furthermore, he was the "head of a gang of ruffianly outlaws" who terrified the Cherokee Nation. Allegedly, Christie had hunted Grinnett down and blown his head almost completely off with a load of buckshot because Grinnett had threatened to inform on the gang.[39]

A report in the *Tahlequah Cherokee Advocate* just a week or so later corrected the previous article, which had blamed Christie for Grinnett's death. According to the *Advocate*, Joe Eagle killed Grinnett when the two got drunk and an old grudge between them reemerged. Not surprisingly, few, if any, newspapers outside Oklahoma picked up on the new story or corrected the old one.[40]

Around sunrise on September 26, 1889, Deputy Marshals Heck Thomas, L.P. Isbell, and three other men went to Christie's home east of Tahlequah and, finding him there, called for his surrender. Christie refused the demand and, instead, climbed into a loft and opened fire on the lawmen. The deputies returned fire, and during the exchange, both Isbell and Christie were seriously wounded. In addition, Christie's cousin's son (often referred to as Christie's son) was shot as he exited the building with Christie's wife. When Christie did not come out as well, the lawmen set fire to the house, but the blaze, too, failed to flush Christie out. The deputies fired a few more shots into the house and then left to seek medical care for Isbell.[41]

The extent of the wounds to Christie and his young kinsman were exaggerated in the press. Initial reports claimed that both the outlaw and the boy were fatally injured. In fact, their wounds were serious but not life threatening, and both recovered fairly quickly.[42]

After the raid on Christie's house failed to kill or capture him, the authorities at Fort Smith issued another indictment against him, and a reward of $500 was offered for his capture. Determined to hold out to the bitter end, Christie built a new bullet-proof home of double logs "right in the middle of his field, with port-holes on every side." No one could approach the place during daytime without being seen, and Christie kept eight or ten dogs that raised a howl if anyone approached at night. Christie also built a ten-foot-high rock fence about a mile east of his home that he used as a lookout for anyone approaching from that direction (i.e., from the direction of Fort Smith). It came to be known as "Ned's Fort."[43]

Newspapers published a number of exaggerated or uncorroborated reports during 1890 and 1891 about Ned Christie's alleged criminal and sometimes violent activities. Calling Christie "as desperate a man… as was ever produced in any country," a report from Fort Smith in early November 1890 recounted a fight he had with the Squirrel brothers, who were fellow Cherokees. The three allegedly got into an argument over a game of "draw." The brothers inflicted three knife wounds on Christie, and he wounded one of them with a gunshot. A sensationalist variation on this story claimed Christie killed the brothers.[44]

In late November 1890, Deputy U.S. Marshal Bass Reeves went out to Christie's place to try to arrest him but didn't find him home. According to at least one report, a frustrated Bass then burned Christie's home/fort to the ground, but this is an obvious error or exaggeration, since Christie continued living there and using it as a fortification after this time. Newspapers suggested that the incident only infuriated Christie, causing him to "go on the warpath" and vow revenge against Reeves. Sure enough, in January 1891, a report filtered out of Fort Smith that Christie had killed Reeves when the legendary Black lawman went out again to try to arrest him—never mind that Bass Reeves lived another twenty years after Christie supposedly killed him.[45]

On June 2, 1891, Deputy Marshals Milo Creekmore and Joe Bowden went out looking for Christie and found him at his home about twelve miles east of Tahlequah. When they approached the place, according to a report from Fort Smith the next day, Christie "stepped out with an ugly-looking Winchester in his grasp and opened fire on the officers." The deputies returned fire, but several friends of Christie came to his aid. "Seeing that the odds were against them," Creekmore and Bowden "sought safety in flight."[46]

Later in June, Bowden's bullet-riddled body was supposedly found south of Tahlequah, and Christie was widely blamed for the killing. Come to find out, though, the person who was killed, if indeed a body was found, was apparently not Bowden. The *Tahlequah Cherokee Advocate* stated as much a week or two after the body was reportedly found and then went on to explain:

> *As this is the age of wonders and wonderful occurrences…it may be, after all, Bowden was killed and that the Bowden we see perambulating the*

streets of Tahlequah is the ghost of Bowden materialized. As we have never been a very stout believer in a fellow coming back after he has passed over the river, we are of the opinion that Bowden was not killed, and that the Marshal Bowden we see rustling around is not a materialized spirit. If he is, he has certainly broken the record in the materializing business.[47]

Not much was heard from or about Ned Christie for the next year. Then on the morning of October 12, 1892 (at least one source says October 11), Deputy Marshal Creekmore, three other deputy marshals, and a posse that included John Fields and Joe Bowers surrounded Christie's home around the break of day. When Creekmore called for Christie to surrender, "the only answer was a deadly volley poured from the loop holes of the cabin fort."[48]

During the exchange of gunfire, Fields was either mortally wounded or killed outright, depending on which of the initial reports one reads, and Bowers was seriously wounded. During the ensuing lull, the lawmen called for the women and children to come out. They complied and were placed under guard. The deputies set some outbuildings on fire in the hopes that the flames would spread to Christie's double-log home, but the plan failed. The lawmen then tried to employ dynamite, but the fuse failed to ignite.[49]

While the other deputies and posse men held Christie at bay, Creekmore hurried to Tahlequah, where he wired Fort Smith for reinforcements. He also gathered a posse in Tahlequah, including local sheriff's deputies, and

NED CHRISTIE.

Characteristic End of a Desperate Outlaw.

RIDDLED WITH BULLETS.

The Deputies Dynamite and Fire His Cabin and Shoot Him as He Runs Out— One of the Gang a Prisoner and the Other Dead and Burned in the Ruins.

Headline proclaims Ned Christie's death. *From the* Oklahoma State Capital.

Ned Christi, noted Cherokee Indian killer, slain by Capt. White and posse, in Spavinaw Hills, C. N.

Opposite: Ned Christie, photographed after he was killed. *Western History Collections, Special Research Collections, University of Oklahoma Libraries, N.H. Rose Collection, image no. 2064.*

Above: The deputies who killed Ned Christie pose for a picture. *Oklahoma Historical Society.*

started back to Christie's place. By the time the reinforcements arrived, however, the first party of lawmen had set fire to Christie's home, flushing him out, but he had managed to escape.[50]

As was often the case where Christie was concerned, the initial reports proved erroneous. Although Fields was shot through the neck, perforating his windpipe, he eventually recovered, as did Bowers.[51]

On the night of November 2, 1892, U.S. Marshal Jacob Yoes and a posse of about twelve men (some sources say as many as fifty) approached and surrounded Christie's home east of Tahlequah. At daylight on November 3, Arch Wolfe, a compadre of Christie, emerged from the house and was ordered to surrender. Instead, he opened fire, and when the marshal's party returned fire, Wolfe was shot twice. He managed, however, to retreat into the house. During the initial exchange of gunfire, Christie sent the women and children who were with him out of the house through a root cellar. The fight then settled into a daylong siege. At one point, Christie's young son was intercepted and detained as he was trying to sneak two boxes of cartridges back into the house for his father.[52]

Neither side suffered any damage during the daytime standoff. The lawmen fired a cannon, which had been sent from Coffeyville, several times, but the projectiles only bounced off the sturdy log house. When the officers tried using a heavier load in the cannon, it blew apart. Late in the evening, the deputies resorted to deploying dynamite. Using a wagon fortified with long rails as a barricade, one of the deputies sneaked up to the house and placed a stick of dynamite under one corner of the building. After he lit the fuse and retreated, a giant explosion that was reportedly heard thirty miles away lifted the cabin off the ground and let it back down.[53]

The explosion blew a hole in the house and set it on fire. Christie crawled out from beneath the floor of the burning structure and made a run for it. When he disregarded a call to halt, he was cut down in a hail of bullets. He made two attempts to rise, but another volley of gunfire from the deputies finished him off. Charles Hair, a young man who worked for Christie, emerged from the burning house shortly after Christie's dash of death, and he was taken into custody with serious burns to his body. Most reports at the time said Arch Wolfe's body was found inside the house, burned to a crisp, but in reality, Wolfe also emerged from the house and was arrested. He and Hair were charged with assault with intent to kill. They were later convicted and sentenced to prison.[54]

Christie's body was taken to Fort Smith for identification and then released to his father for burial in the family cemetery at Wauhillau, Oklahoma. Since his death, Christie has often been sensationally depicted in books and articles as a violent, bloodthirsty desperado, just as he was sometimes represented during his life. On the other hand, at least one story emerged in the early 1900s purporting to exonerate Christie completely of the Maples murder, the crime that catapulted him into outlawry, and many Cherokees today honor him as a hero for standing against U.S. government encroachment on tribal properties and rights.[55]

4

BOB ROGERS

A DESPERATE OUTLAW AND A RECKLESS VILLAIN

Afterr Bob Rogers was killed near Nowata by a posse sent out to arrest him on the early morning of March 16, 1895, a Coffeyville, Kansas newspaper described him as "the notorious chief of what is known as the Rogers gang of thieves and bold bandits, a murderous band that has infested the Northern part of the Cherokee Nation for upward of two years." Two years, however, might be a low estimate of how far back Rogers's life of outlawry stretched.[56]

Born around 1873 in Arkansas, Bob, who was part Cherokee, moved to the Nowata area of Indian Territory with his father, Frank, and younger brothers, Sam and Jim, when he was still a boy. Some sources say he embarked on his career of crime in the fall of 1891 at the age of eighteen when he was arrested for assault with intent to kill. After he was taken to Fort Smith, he was promptly released on bond. Back home in Indian Territory, young Rogers started gathering around him other desperate young men, including Bob Stiteler, Willis Brown, "Dynamite Jack" Turner, and Turner's brother "Kiowa" Turner. The gang was arrested in the summer of 1892 on suspicion of stealing horses in the Cherokee Nation and selling them in Arkansas. All five gang members were escorted to Fort Smith, where Rogers was initially sentenced to the federal reformatory before he was pardoned on account of his youth.[57]

Details about these early outlaw escapades of Rogers, however, are scant to nonexistent. Rogers's first criminal exploit that was well documented occurred on November 3, 1892, when he killed forty-year-old Jess W. Elliott at Catoosa. Elliott was a Cherokee lawyer who had traveled from Vinita to Catoosa on business, and Rogers, going by the name Bob Talton, had been working on a ranch at Catoosa. On the fateful day, both men had been drinking when they fell in with each other at a billiard parlor in Catoosa and got into an argument. Rogers knocked Elliott down and commenced beating him. Bystanders separated the two men, ushering Rogers out of the room and holding Elliott inside. When Elliott was finally turned loose, he got on his horse and started riding up the street. Rogers, who had been waiting for Elliott, followed and knocked him off the horse. He then cut the older man's throat with a knife, "making three horrible gashes," and left him in the street to bleed to death. Someone who was passing by saw Elliott leaning against a post and heard his blood gushing out but thought the unfortunate man was vomiting. The wounded man was dead by time medical help arrived.[58]

The attending doctor and other bystanders built a fire near the body and stayed to watch it, but Rogers showed back up a couple of hours later, rode through the fire, and ran the onlookers off. He then "kicked and stamped the lifeless body of his victim, put on and wore his hat for a while, looked through the papers in his pocket and then left."[59]

A posse organized and started in pursuit of Rogers but failed to overtake him. The fugitive was last heard from at Sapulpa, where he left word that he was headed west.[60]

Eight months later, the Bob Rogers gang, which now included Rogers's younger brothers, robbed the Frisco Depot at Chelsea, Oklahoma, of $418 on the evening of June 30, 1893. Some sources credit this exploit to Henry Starr, but that seems unlikely, since Starr was arrested at a hotel in Colorado just three days later.[61]

Around noon on July 13, Rogers and two partners in crime robbed the Mound Valley Bank in Kansas. They bound and gagged the cashier and made off with about $800. In the immediate wake of the crime, some people again dubiously credited the Starr gang with the caper.[62]

These criminal activities put U.S. marshals on the trail of the Rogers gang, and on July 30, Deputy Marshal Heck Bruner and a posse intercepted part of the gang at a farm about ten miles southwest of Vinita. In the ensuing shootout, Ralph Halleck was killed and Sam Rogers severely wounded. Before he died, Halleck admitted he had participated in the Mound Valley Bank robbery, and he was also identified as one of the men who'd held up the depot at Chelsea.[63]

On the evening of Friday, October 20, two men entered the depot of the DM&A Railroad at Edna, Kansas, and forced the agent at the point

Deputy Heck Bruner, who hunted for and fought with the Bob Rogers gang. *Oklahoma Historical Society.*

of a revolver to open the safe. Recognized as Bob Rogers and Dick Brown of "the Wooten-Rogers gang of outlaws," the men made off with about fifty dollars. They were not disguised and showed no concern about being recognized. However, they were not pursued into Indian Territory because "Edna is so close to the Territory line and the country south of that point is so constituted that it is a very difficult matter for officers to follow criminals into it without needlessly endangering their lives at the hands of the fellows who infest that locality."[64]

An outlaw gang tried to hold up a Missouri, Kansas and Texas train at the Kelso switch about six miles northeast of Vinita on December 22, 1893. The robbery attempt failed when the engineer sped the train through the siding, but a member of the train crew was shot and wounded by the bandits. The escapade was later credited to the Rogers gang.[65]

Bob Rogers and his crew struck again two nights later on Christmas Eve, when they held up an Iron Mountain Railroad train at Seminole in Indian Territory, about five miles south of Coffeyville, Kansas. A report from Coffeyville published in a Wichita newspaper described what happened. As the train approached the station, it was flagged by five young men. One of the gang guarded the engineer while the other four went through the train "securing valuables of every description." The mail and express cars were "cleaned out," and "every passenger on the train was relieved of everything of value he had." The outlaws kept up a sporadic stream of revolver fire throughout the duration of the robbery, which lasted over an hour.[66]

The bandits were described as young men who dressed like cowboys, "wearing top boots and broad brimmed hats." Bob Rogers and Charley Wooten were thought to be the leaders of the gang. U.S. Deputy Marshal Heck Bruner left Coffeyville on Christmas Day with "a strong posse" in pursuit of the robbers, but "as they have friends in the territory who will keep them posted of the movements of the officers, shield, provide them with food and protect them while they are hiding, their capture will be a difficult matter."[67]

In early January 1894, Bob Rogers's youngest brother, James, and another member of the Rogers gang named Carmile Redingbird held up the Hayden store in the Indian Territory, just a few miles south of Coffeyville. They were tracked down and arrested a few days later. Redingbird was identified as one of the gang that had robbed the train at Seminole on Christmas Eve, and young Rogers was identified as the brother of Bob Rogers, "a well known and dangerous criminal and fugitive from justice."[68]

On January 7, Deputy Marshal W.C. Smith made a raid on the home of Bob Rogers's brother-in-law Henry Daniels, surprising Rogers and Bob Stiteler, who were spending the night there. Both men were captured, but Rogers quickly escaped, while Stiteler was taken to Fort Smith. Later, it was alleged that Rogers had betrayed Stiteler to the lawmen for the reward money.[69]

In the early morning of January 23, U.S. deputy marshals surprised the Rogers gang at the home of Frank Rogers on Big Creek between Vinita and Nowata. Bob Rogers and Dynamite Jack Turner were captured unhurt and without a fight, but Dynamite's brother Kiowa was killed outright and Willis Brown was mortally wounded when they engaged the deputies in gunplay. None of the officers was hurt. Commenting on the raid, the *Coffeyville Weekly Journal* opined, "The dreadful work of a few minutes ends the career of four puny emulators of the James's [*sic*] and Daltons, one dead, one dying and three in prison."[70]

Well, no, Bob Rogers's career wasn't quite at an end.

After he was taken to Fort Smith, Rogers was released on bond. When he returned home, the *Coffeyville Weekly Journal* commented, either mistakenly or facetiously, that Bob Rogers had been given a commission as a U.S. deputy marshal. And the *Vinita Weekly Chieftain* complained that an ordinary citizen would be arrested for wearing a gun in Vinita but said that, on the night of Saturday, March 31, Bob Rogers was packing a pistol and walking the streets with impunity.[71]

The newspapers were right to be skeptical of the lenient treatment Rogers had apparently received. In early October 1894, all the charges against him were dropped in exchange for him turning state's evidence against the other members of the gang, but that didn't stop him from promptly reorganizing a new outlaw gang. By very early March 1895, the new Rogers gang had already committed "several small depredations" in the area of Nowata and, according to the *Coffeyville Daily Journal*, were "but waiting for a favorable opportunity of holding up a train or a bank."[72]

Indeed, the day after the *Daily Journal* reported the reorganization of the Rogers gang, the same newspaper reported that a store at Angola, Kansas, along with its customers, had been held up by two masked, heavily armed men and that the robbers were thought to be Bob Rogers and Bill Elsmore. The very next day, the same Coffeyville paper confirmed the identification of the two holdup men.[73]

Rogers's new notoriety didn't last long. On the evening of Friday, March 15, U.S. Marshal James Mayes learned that Rogers and his recent sidekick, Elsmore, were holed up at Rogers's father's home on Big Creek. Mayes, with a posse composed of citizens from the neighborhood, surrounded the Rogers home early Saturday morning. A man who lived on the Rogers place awakened and informed the posse that Elsmore had left but that Rogers and his father were upstairs.[74]

Hearing the commotion, Frank Rogers came downstairs, and Marshal Mayes called up to Bob that he had a warrant for his arrest. He assured the desperado that if he would come down with his hands up, he would not be hurt. Rogers defiantly refused the invitation and challenged the posse to come and take him.[75]

On orders from the posse, Old Man Rogers then led the way up the stairs, with two or three posse members close behind. The whole party had not yet reached the room where Bob Rogers was holed up when the outlaw opened fire, killing a posse man named McDaniel and wounding another. The posse retreated, bringing their wounded partner and Frank Rogers along, but they were forced to leave the dead man where he fell.[76]

From outside the house, the posse once again called on Rogers to surrender, threatening to burn the house down around him if he did not comply. He finally offered to come out if they would let him keep his rifle in his hands. They agreed under the condition that he carry the weapon at his side with the muzzle down.

Instead of carrying his Winchester at his side with one hand and pointed down, as the posse expected, Rogers emerged from the house carrying the

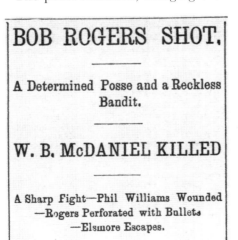

BOB ROGERS SHOT.

A Determined Posse and a Reckless Bandit.

W. B. McDANIEL KILLED

A Sharp Fight—Phil Williams Wounded —Rogers Perforated with Bullets —Elsmore Escapes.

Headline announces the death of Bob Rogers. *From the* Coffeyville (KS) Daily Journal.

rifle at his hip with both hands. From their hiding places, the posse members did not have a clear view of the outlaw at first, and they began parlaying with him. He refused to throw up his hands as they instructed and, instead, began backing toward the door through which he had come. When he caught a glimpse of Marshal Mayes, he quickly raised his rifle to fire, but he got off just one shot before "a half dozen rifles uttered their messages of death, and the reckless bandit fell riddled with bullets." At the same time, Rogers's shot merely grazed the marshal's head.[77]

Rogers's body was turned over to his father, while McDaniel's body was taken to his nearby home and handed over to his loved ones. The *Coffeyville Daily Journal* concluded that the death of McDaniel and the wounding of the other posse member were "the only features of the affair that will cause regret. The death of Rogers will rid the country of a desperate outlaw and reckless villain."[78]

5

HENRY STARR AND THE MURDER OF DEPUTY MARSHAL FLOYD WILSON

Henry Starr boasted that he had robbed more banks "than any man in America" during a notorious career that spanned thirty years from the early 1890s to the early 1920s. While many of those bank holdups occurred outside Starr's native northeast Oklahoma, his murder of Deputy Marshal Floyd Wilson early in his criminal career happened in his home territory near Nowata. He didn't brag about that crime.

Starr was born near Fort Gibson in 1873 in the Cherokee Nation. The son of George "Hop" and Mary Scott Starr, he was a nephew by marriage of Belle Starr, the so-called Bandit Queen. Henry's grandfather Tom Starr was a noted outlaw in his own right. After Henry's father died in 1886 and his mother remarried a few months later, Henry went to stay with relatives because he didn't get along with his stepfather. In 1888, Henry and the relatives he was living with moved north to the Nowata area of the Cherokee Nation.[79]

Henry Starr had his first run-in with the law in December 1891, when he was accused of horse stealing. He was arrested and taken to jail at Fort Smith, but the charge was dropped. Upon his return to Nowata, he soon got into trouble again when he was caught driving a wagon that contained whiskey, and he was charged with "introducing spirits" into Indian Territory. He was released on bond when the ranchers he was working for signed for him, but he eventually paid a fine of $100. Starr claimed he was totally innocent of both charges. The supposedly unfair charges and the unpleasant experiences attached to each soured Starr against the law, and he decided that if he was going to be treated like a criminal, he might as well become one.[80]

In May 1892, Starr was arrested for stealing horses near Claremore and again taken to jail at Fort Smith. He was bailed out by his uncle Judge Watt Starr and Chief Harris of the Cherokee tribe.[81]

After Starr was released, he forfeited his bond and went on a criminal spree, as he later admitted. The Missouri Pacific Railroad agent at Nowata and two travelers were held up one night in August 1892, and the holdup was laid at the feet of Henry Starr and a sidekick named Ed Newcomb. In late October or early November that same year, Starr and one or two other men held up the H.C. Schufeldt General Store at Lenapah, Indian Territory. The victim of the nighttime crime, young John Schufeldt, said he didn't know the robbers, and he refused to give a description, apparently afraid they would come back and harm him if he did. Then the John W. Carter store at Sequoyah, Indian Territory, was held up in mid-November in broad daylight. The robbers walked in and found Carter's clerk in the store alone. They presented their Winchesters and forced him to turn over all the cash on hand. The bandits walked out with about $575 and "made themselves scarce." The men who executed the latest robbery were said to be the same men who had held up the Missouri Pacific agent at Nowata and robbed John Schufeldt at Lenapah only a few days earlier.[82]

In early December 1892, the Missouri Pacific Railroad sent Special Agent H.C. Dickey out from St. Louis to hunt down the men who'd robbed the agent at Nowata. Dickey recruited a partner, Deputy Marshal Floyd Wilson, at Fort Smith, and the two men arrived in Nowata on Sunday, December 11. They left Nowata that evening, ranging north toward Lenapah, and searched several places where they thought Starr might be. Failing to find him, they laid over at Arthur Dodge's ranch near present-day Delaware from Monday morning through Tuesday morning, hoping to see Starr pass by on his way to see his sister, who lived nearby.[83]

Around 1:00 p.m. on Tuesday, they saw Starr headed in a southeasterly direction. Wilson mounted the only saddled horse available and started after Starr, leaving the ranch manager to saddle a horse for Dickey. After Wilson had chased Starr for about a mile, Starr recognized Wilson's horse and, thinking the rider was one of Dodge's cowboys, stopped to wait. When Wilson rode up and covered Starr with his Winchester, Starr sprang from his horse as if to make a stand. As soon as Wilson dismounted, though, Starr jumped back on his horse and galloped off. Wilson remounted and resumed the pursuit. After a short distance, both men dismounted again, ready for a fight.[84]

Henry Starr. *Oklahoma Historical Society.*

Wilson fired one shot at Starr before "his Winchester hung." He tossed the rifle aside, drew his pistol, and rolled around on the ground to continue the fight. Starr returned fire, wounding Wilson in the leg. The outlaw advanced on the prostrate deputy marshal, shooting him several more times. Starr was allegedly just four or five feet away when he fired the last shot into Wilson's body.[85]

Dickey rode up and dismounted around this time, and Starr fired his last three rifle shots at him. Dickey fired one or two shots at Starr, who grabbed Wilson's discarded rifle and tried to make it work but couldn't. He then drew his pistol and got off a couple of more shots at Dickey before he leaped onto Wilson's horse. Both Starr's and Dickey's horses had run away during the gun battle, allowing the outlaw to ride away unmolested.[86]

Dickey took his comrade's dead body into nearby Coffeyville, Kansas, just across the state line. From there, it was transported by train to Fort Smith.[87]

After Wilson's death, authorities redoubled their efforts to run Henry Starr to ground. A false report circulated in late December, just weeks after the Wilson killing, that Starr had been captured near Talala, Indian Territory, but it proved to be a canard. In mid-January 1893, deputies skirmished with members of the Starr gang near Bartlesville, but Starr himself either escaped or was not present.[88]

The fact that officers were hot on Starr's trail hardly slowed his criminal spree. In the space of a little over three months, he robbed two banks and a train and was rumored to have pulled off a few other jobs.

In late March 1893, Starr and his sidekick Frank Cheney robbed the First National Bank of Caney, Kansas, and made off with almost $5,000.[89]

On the night of May 2, six unmasked bandits, "supposed to be the notorious Starr gang," held up an MKT (Missouri, Kansas and Texas) passenger train at Pryor Creek, Indian Territory, in present-day Mayes County. When a bend in the road forced the train to slow, six men emerged from some timber with Winchesters in hand and signaled the train to stop. The gang rounded up several railroad employees, and while two of the gang guarded the prisoners, other members of the gang entered the express car. They threatened the messenger with pistols, but he adamantly insisted he could not open the large "through" safe. The gang finally satisfied themselves with the smaller "local" safe, which yielded some jewelry and a few other items. The gang members then started relieving individual employees and passengers of their money and valuables. According to at least one report, they punctuated their work with about forty shots fired into the air. When they were ready to leave, the outlaws marched some of their captives down the tracks to where they'd tied their horses, mounted up, and rode away. Estimates of their take varied from just a small amount to over $2,000. One newspaper said simply, "Everything worth having was appropriated by the bandits."[90]

BOLDER THAN THE DALTON GANG.

The Pryor Creek Train Robbers Wore No Masks.

Express Messenger Sproule Couldn't Open the Big Safe and the Bandits Didn't Get Its Contents—Exciting Experiences of Train- men and Pas- sengers.

Newspaper report of the Pryor Creek train robbery. *From the* St. Louis Globe- Democrat.

A month later, in early June, the gang robbed the People's Bank of Bentonville, Arkansas, making off with over $10,000.[91]

Another month later, Starr and a member of his gang, Kid Wilson, were apprehended in Colorado. Starr was arrested on the morning of July 3 at a hotel in Colorado Springs, where he had stayed the night before with a young woman who claimed to be his wife. Later the same morning, officers nabbed Wilson at Colorado City. Wilson, too, had stayed at the Colorado Springs hotel the night before, and all three had registered under assumed names. Starr and the young woman had checked in as Mr. and Mrs. Frank Jackson of Joplin, Missouri, and the "Kid" gave his name as John Wilson, also of Joplin.[92]

Described as being about eighteen years old and "rather prepossessing," the young woman said she'd been married to Starr for several months and that her home was about two hundred miles east of Colorado. The woman was carrying a pearl-handled .38-caliber revolver, and a search of her and Starr's room turned up about $500 in gold and $1,500 in greenbacks.[93]

After Starr was brought back to Fort Smith to face numerous charges, a romantic embellishment about how the young woman and the outlaw met was added to the girl's already-quixotic tale. According to a report that was published when Starr's trial for the murder of Wilson began in the fall of 1893, the young woman, whose name was Mary Smith, was among the passengers on the first coach of the train that the Starr gang held up at Pryor Creek. When Starr mounted the platform of the car, Mary jumped from the coach and fled in terror into the darkness. When the holdup was over and the gang was riding away, they came upon the young woman, who was wandering in the woods and crazed with fear, a short distance from the railroad. Starr took her on his horse to the outlaw camp, and she soon became attached to him. Their affection for each other grew warm, and Starr sent Mary home to Joplin, promising to follow her there and marry her. When he showed up a few weeks later, Mary's parents gave their consent, and Starr wed the young lady under the name Frank Jackson. Starr later dismissed the newspaper stories about Mary as sensationalist journalism. He said Mary was from the Nowata area and that they had been sweethearts for several years; he said they had planned to get married when they reached the West Coast.[94]

In the fall of 1893, Starr was convicted of murdering Wilson, and Judge Isaac Parker (i.e., the hanging judge) sentenced him to death. The verdict was overturned on appeal. A second trial resulted in a similar verdict, but again, Starr's lawyers won a new trial for their client. At Starr's third trial in January 1898, the defense negotiated a plea bargain deal that resulted in a sentence for Starr of only fifteen years in prison.[95]

Considered a model prisoner, Starr had his sentence commuted by President Theodore Roosevelt, and he was released in 1903. He tried to go straight for a while, but when Arkansas authorities began trying to extradite him for the Bentonville bank robbery, he soon relapsed into his old ways. He, Kid Wilson, and another man held up a bank at Tyro, Kansas, on March 13, 1908, and then exchanged gunfire near Wann later the same day with lawmen who chased them into Oklahoma.[96]

Starr eluded his pursuers and headed west. In July 1908, he and Kid Wilson held up a bank at Amity, Colorado. Starr fled the state but was arrested in Arizona in May 1909 and brought back to Colorado. Found guilty of the Amity bank robbery, Starr was sentenced to a long stint in a Colorado prison, but he was paroled for good behavior in 1913.[97]

Starr worked for a while in Colorado before drifting back to Oklahoma, where he soon went on another criminal rampage. In the space of just four months, from September 1914 to January 1915, no fewer than fourteen bank robberies across the state of Oklahoma were attributed to Starr. Then in March 1915, Starr and six sidekicks attempted to rob two banks at once in Stroud, Oklahoma. Armed citizens engaged the robbers in a gunfight, and Starr and another gang member were wounded and captured during the shootout. However, the gang avoided a reenactment of the Dalton gang's 1892 fiasco at Coffeyville because the other four outlaws made off with almost $6,000.[98]

Starr pleaded guilty to the Stroud bank robbery and was sentenced to spend twenty-five years in the Oklahoma State Prison at McAlester. After serving four years, he was paroled by the governor in March 1919.[99]

After his release, Starr joined a motion picture company and made a silent movie based on the Stroud caper called *A Debtor to the Law*. Apparently, though, Starr decided he like being an outlaw better than playing one in the movies. In February 1921, he and three sidekicks held up a bank in Harrison, Arkansas, and Starr was mortally wounded during the robbery. He died a few hours later, and his body was taken back to Dewey, Oklahoma, for burial.[100]

6

CHEROKEE BILL AND THE BILL COOK GANG

alled by one historian "one of the most famous outlaws in the history of the Indian Territory" and by another "probably the most famous outlaw that was hanged on the Fort Smith gallows," Crawford Goldsby, alias Cherokee Bill, was born in Texas in 1876. His father, George Goldsby, was a mixed-race Buffalo Soldier, and his mother, Ellen Beck, was half Black, one-fourth white and one-fourth Cherokee.[101]

After George Goldsby deserted Ellen, she returned with her family to her home at Fort Gibson (Indian Territory). Young Crawford Goldsby grew up there, except for time spent in Native schools in Kansas and Pennsylvania. As a teenager, he worked odds jobs around Fort Gibson before his first run-in with the law when he was just seventeen.[102]

In the fall of 1893, Goldsby attended a "negro dance" in Fort Gibson, and a disturbance arose between him and a man named Jake Lewis, reportedly over a young girl whom Goldsby was struck on. Lewis "gave the boy a whipping," and a few days later, on the morning of October 31, Goldsby armed himself and went looking for Lewis. When he found him at a stable feeding stock, Goldsby opened fire. Lewis started running, but three shots struck him in the back. It was reported at the time that the wounds were fatal, but Lewis lived to file charges against the young man.[103]

Shortly after this incident, Goldsby, now going by the name Cherokee Bill, joined the Bill Cook gang. At first, the gang's illegal activities were relatively minor offenses, like running whiskey, but they soon escalated to more serious crimes. Goldsby and Cook were mentioned for one of the first times together in the newspapers in early July 1894. Two deputy U.S. marshals were on their way to Fort Smith with three prisoners, who were charged with horse stealing and selling liquor illegally. When the party camped near Sapulpa, Goldsby and Cook sent two notes to the marshals, warning the lawmen that they should stay away from them or be killed. One of the notes was signed "W.T. Cook," and the other one was signed "Cherokee Bill."[104]

Later in July, the Cook gang held up a Frisco passenger train at Red Fork, Indian Territory. The desperadoes overpowered the express agent, knocked him in the head, and ransacked the express car, but the heist "resulted in very little money to the bandits" and the agent was not seriously hurt.[105]

On July 30, the gang rode into Chandler and robbed the Lincoln County Bank in broad daylight. A barber named Mitchell, who was seated in front of his shop diagonally across the street from the bank, cried out, "The Daltons are here!" He was warned to be quiet, but as he rose to go inside, he repeated his outcry and was shot and killed by one of the gang members. An outlaw named Lucas was wounded and captured during the holdup, and he told the sheriff that Bill Cook and Cherokee Bill were among the other gang members.[106]

On September 16, a deputy U.S. marshal went into an outlaw camp in the Creek Nation, just south of the Cherokee line, under a flag of truce. Most of the outlaws were members of the Cook gang, but Bill Doolin and other Dalton gang veterans were among those in the camp. The lawman tried to talk the desperadoes into giving up bank and train robbery, but they told him they had "gone too far to turn back now."[107]

The next day, September 17, four members of the Cook gang robbed the J.A. Parkinson store in Okmulgee at gunpoint. They took about $450 in cash and some goods from the store. They returned some checks and other nonnegotiable notes and gave back a coat that didn't fit any of the bandits. Bill Cook, who grew up at Okmulgee, was recognized by a number of witnesses.[108]

On the evening of October 9, three members of the Cook gang held up the Valley Depot at Claremore "in true and approved Territory style." The night operator, M.M. Lott, had his chair tilted back with his hat lowered over his eyes when he was startled by the sound of gunshots and breaking glass. He awoke to find the barrel of a Winchester staring him in the face. Although discombobulated by the interruption, he "had the presence of mind to shove up his hands when commanded to do so," according to a Claremore newspaper. Another employee, station agent Patrick, was ordered to clean out the safe, which "he could hardly refuse to do and still retain his usual health." The gang made off with about fifty dollars and took two bystanders along as hostages. At the edge of town, they released the two men and told them they could go back into town. The outlaws were identified as members of the Cook gang because they had been seen in the vicinity earlier in the day and had robbed a couple of men on the road. Two hours after the Claremore stickup, the same gang reportedly robbed the depot at Chouteau over twenty miles away.[109]

In late October, when it was rumored that the federal government was about to place a $1,000 reward on the heads of Bill Cook and his gang, an Oklahoma City newspaper gave its readers some background on Cook and how his gang came about:

> *Cook is the successor of Bill Dalton, and when that worthy died, Cook gathered about the remnants of the band of outlaws and, adding to it some of his own associates, has now a gang that is more lawless and daring than any that has ever operated in the southwest since the days of Jesse and Frank James. Cook himself, who is only 24 years old, is more daring and reckless than Dalton ever was, and has committed deeds in his brief career of which Dalton would never have dreamed.*[110]

The rumored reward was issued a few days later, and five thousand posters were distributed throughout the section of Indian Territory that the Cook gang was known to inhabit. Cherokee Bill, in addition to Cook, was among those mentioned by name on the poster. The Cook gang was now wanted dead or alive, but as one reporter pointed out, the outlaws would not be easy to capture or kill because they were well armed, knew the territory well, and had many sympathizers who would take their side against any government agents who came looking for them.[111]

Shortly after the reward was offered, another article giving additional details about the Cook gang circulated in newspapers. The article identified Cherokee Bill as the "first lieutenant" of the gang. He was also considered "the best shot and the most dangerous member." The description continued:

> *He handles a Winchester with the rapidity of lightning. He shoots by the angle system and never takes time to catch sight along the barrel of his gun. He shoots on the same principle that one would throw a stone at an object. He seldom or never misses his mark. He killed several men before he joined Cook and large rewards are offered for his body, dead or alive.*[112]

BILL COOK.

Left: Crawford Goldsby (alias Cherokee Bill). *Oklahoma Historical Society.*

Right: Bill Cook, the leader of Cherokee Bill's gang. *From the* Carlisle (PA) Evening Herald.

In the early afternoon of November 9, 1894, Cherokee Bill and another man rode into the small village of Lenapah, about ten miles north of Nowata, and held up the Schufeldt store. Standing at the front door, Cherokee Bill kept the proprietor and his clerk covered "while the other bandit went through the victims in the most approved style," taking a gold watch and about $100 from Schufeldt and a small amount of money from the clerk. As the bandits were walking out, Cherokee Bill spotted a young man, later identified as Ernest Melton, at a window of a restaurant adjoining the store. He immediately raised his rifle and fired through a glass window, striking Melton in the eye and killing him instantly. As the two desperadoes rode out of town, they fired a shot at Schufeldt's wife when they spotted her looking out an upstairs window of the store, but the shot missed its mark. They also fired a few other shots into the air to "intimidate the citizens" as they rode away.[113]

A mile or so southwest of Lenapah, the two outlaws shot a horse "just for fun." A few miles farther on, they stole two horses to replace their own. Even though the law was notified of the holdup and murder in time to chase after the perpetrators, "nobody seemed anxious to catch them," according to a Coffeyville newspaper.[114]

On the night of November 16, a posse of deputy marshals trapped Cherokee Bill and two companions in a home a few miles west of Talala. They realized they were surrounded when a horse belonging to one of the deputies neighed loudly, so Cherokee Bill and his small gang burst through the door and engaged the lawmen in a fierce gunfight. Cherokee Bill was "hit three times and knocked down twice by Winchester bullets," according to a resident of Talala, "but each time recovered his feet" and finally reached his horse and made his escape with his two sidekicks. The man from Talala thought Cherokee Bill must have been wearing a steel corselet to have made such a miraculous escape.[115]

Two days later, a man happened to meet Cherokee Bill on the road between Claremore and Tahlequah, and the two engaged in conversation. Cherokee Bill made no effort to conceal his identity and talked freely about the Talala fight. He seemed elated over his escape, showed off his wounds, and joked that he was going to have to "lay up" for a while to recuperate. He had bound his own wounds, explaining that he didn't trust doctors. Cherokee Bill had a traveling companion, who had been with him at Talala, but he said his other partner in the Talala fight had deserted them at first fire.[116]

On the evening of Saturday, December 22, while Bill Cook was laid up from the wounds he'd suffered in a shootout with lawmen, Cherokee Bill and several other men held up the train depot in Nowata. Approaching the platform outside the depot, three gunmen covered the station agent with Winchesters and ordered him inside. Cherokee Bill, who was recognized as the leader of the small gang, ordered his two companions to keep a sharp lookout so he could "attend to this business." Cherokee Bill ordered the agent to "shell out," and the railroad man promptly anted up eighty dollars in cash and a gold watch. After they got all there was to get, Cherokee Bill stepped outside and fired five shots into the air. Three other gang members quickly rode up leading three extra horses; the three men at the station mounted up, and the whole gang rode away.[117]

On Saturday, December 29, Cherokee Bill, in company with his brother-in-law, Mose Brown, visited the home of Frank Daniels, a Black man living a few miles west of Talala. Trouble had been brewing for some time between Cherokee Bill and Brown over Brown's alleged ill treatment of Bill's sister. While at the Daniels residence, Bill and his brother-in-law went to a grove of trees a few hundred yards south of the house, with Bill riding his horse and Brown walking alongside. After a heated conversation between the two men, Brown started back toward the house. He paused and appeared, to those watching from the house, to be pleading with Cherokee Bill, but Bill waved him off and ordered him to "move faster." Brown started up again but had gone only a few steps when Cherokee Bill raised his rifle and fired three shots into the retreating figure. Brown fell dead, but Bill dismounted and shot him twice more. Still not satisfied, the murderer rolled Brown's corpse over and fired two more bullets into it. Leaving Brown's body to "make food for the coyotes," Cherokee Bill remounted, exchanged a few words with the occupants of the house, and rode away.[118]

"Anxious to crowd all the crime he could into the old year," Cherokee Bill paid a return visit to the Nowata train depot on the evening of December 31 and single-handedly robbed the same station agent, J.L. Bristow, that he and his sidekicks had held up less than two weeks earlier. Cherokee Bill herded the agent and a hotel porter into the depot at gunpoint, and Bristow quickly handed over the contents of the safe, about thirty-eight dollars. The robber then marched Bristow back outside, bid him "good night" some distance from the depot, and was soon "lost to view in the darkness." Unnerved by the experience, Bristow immediately turned in his resignation.[119]

Lawmen captured Bill Cook in New Mexico on January 12, 1895, after a lengthy pursuit, and the bandit was brought back to the federal jail at Fort Smith, Arkansas. Just a couple of weeks later, ex–U.S. deputy Ike Rogers captured Cherokee Bill at Rogers's home east of Nowata when Cherokee Bill called there to visit a female cousin of Rogers, whom he'd recently

Cherokee Bill (*third from left*) with the posse who brought him to jail. *Oklahoma Historical Society*.

been seeing. Cherokee Bill joined Cook at the U.S. jail in Fort Smith on the evening of January 30.[120]

In mid-February, Bill Cook was found guilty on several charges of robbery and sentenced to forty-five years in prison. Later in the month, Cherokee Bill was also tried and convicted on several counts of robbery. Still later in February, he was tried and convicted for the murder of Ernest Melton, the man he shot during the holdup of Schufeldt's store at Lenapah the previous November. In mid-April, Judge Isaac Parker, the so-called hanging judge, sentenced him to die on the gallows in June, but the sentence was later stayed.[121]

In late July 1895, Cherokee Bill killed guard Larry Keating during an escape attempt at the federal jail in Fort Smith. None other than fellow inmate Henry Starr was credited with inducing Cherokee Bill to give up his weapon after the murder, likely preventing additional bloodshed.[122]

In August, Cherokee Bill was tried and convicted for the murder of Keating, and Parker again sentenced him to hang. This sentence, too, was delayed by appeal, but the fateful day finally came on March 17, 1896, Cherokee Bill died "as indifferent to the world on the gallows" as he had been throughout his life, according to a headline in a Little Rock newspaper. Just before the guard pulled the lever that dropped him into eternity, Cherokee Bill remarked with a smile on his lips, "This is a fine day to die."[123]

7

THE 1921 TULSA RACE MASSACRE

On the morning of Monday, May 30, 1921, Dick Rowland, a nineteen-year-old Black shoe shine, took a break from his job outside the Drexel building in downtown Tulsa, Oklahoma, so that he could go inside and use the segregated restroom on the third floor. Stepping into the elevator, he came face to face with a young white girl, seventeen-year-old Sarah Page, who was operating the elevator.[124]

What happened next is not entirely clear, but according to most sources, Rowland either accidentally stepped on the girl's toe and grabbed her arm to keep her from falling or tripped on the elevator threshold and grabbed her arm to regain his balance. When she screamed for help, Rowland left the scene.[125]

This seemingly benign encounter led to what some have called the worst single incident of racial violence in American history, discounting slavery. Over a period of twelve hours or more from the evening of May 31 until the late morning of June 1, white Tulsans carried out a rampage of terror through the prosperous Black Greenwood District that left at least sixty and some say as many as three hundred Black Americans dead. Well over one thousand businesses and residences were burned, several hundred others were looted but not burned, and thousands of people were left homeless. Often called the Tulsa Race Riot or the Tulsa Race War in the past, the tragedy has come to be known more aptly in recent years as the Tulsa Race Massacre.[126]

When police arrived at the Drexel building to take Miss Page's statement, she told officers that she had screamed because a young Black man had grabbed her. Rowland was arrested the next day at his home on Greenwood Avenue and taken before Miss Page, who identified him as the man who had supposedly attacked her. Charged with assault, Rowland was placed in the city jail. A short time later, he was moved to the county jail at the courthouse in downtown Tulsa. Rowland did not deny that he had grabbed the girl's arm, but he said it was an accident and that he did not scratch her or otherwise molest her. His protestations of innocence made no difference to many Tulsans when they heard of his arrest. In their minds, a Black "demon" had accosted a poor, innocent white girl and, no doubt, intended to rape her. That was all they needed to know.[127]

In the highly charged racial atmosphere of the early 1920s, when the Ku Klux Klan was in the middle of a resurgence, even a relatively nonthreatening encounter between a Black person and a white person could lead to mob violence against Black Americans. This was especially true if the Black person was male and the white person was female. For a young Black man even to associate with a white girl was seen as a challenge to white male authority. The tension was particularly high in Tulsa, where many Black citizens lived in and around the thriving Greenwood Business District, which was known as Black Wall Street because of its economic success. Meanwhile, many poor whites just across the railroad tracks to the south were struggling financially and surely resented their prosperous neighbors.[128]

On the afternoon of Tuesday, May 31, the *Tulsa Tribune* published a front-page article portraying the encounter between Rowland and Page as an attempted rape. The newspaper may have even suggested in a now-lost editorial that a lynching was likely to take place that night. Throughout the afternoon and early evening, rumors of such a lynching were whispered from one white Tulsan to another, and by about 7:30 p.m., hundreds of angry white Tulsans had gathered outside the Tulsa County Courthouse. The mob demanded that law officers turn over Rowland, but Sheriff W.M. McCullough refused.[129]

When word of the impending lynching reached the Greenwood District, Black citizens were determined to not let it happen. About twenty-five armed men, some of them World War I veterans, drove to the courthouse around 9:00 p.m. and offered to help defend Rowland should the gathering mob decide to take the law into their own hands. Assured that Rowland was in no danger and that the situation was under control, they returned to Greenwood.[130]

The appearance of armed Black men at the courthouse alarmed and angered the white mob. Some of those who didn't already have weapons went home to get them. One group of white men tried to break into the National Guard armory to retrieve weapons but were repelled by national guardsmen. By 9:30 p.m., the mob had grown to about two thousand. McCullough tried to talk the mob into dispersing, but the crowd hooted him down.[131]

Around 10:00 p.m., a rumor reached the Greenwood District that white Tulsans were storming the courthouse, and a second group of Black men, perhaps as many as seventy-five, went to the courthouse to offer their help in maintaining order, but again they were turned away. As the Black men were leaving, a white man accosted one of them and tried to disarm him. The Black man, a World War I veteran, refused to hand over his weapon. During the ensuing struggle, a shot was fired, and the riot was on.[132]

The white mob opened fire on the Black men, and they returned fire. Estimates of the number killed in this initial exchange vary widely, from one to twenty or more. Greatly outnumbered, the Black men retreated toward the Greenwood District, skirmishing with a pursuing horde of white men along the way. Intense fighting broke out along Fourth Street sometime before midnight, and an even deadlier gunfight erupted at Second Street and Cincinnati Avenue shortly after midnight.[133]

Meanwhile, at the courthouse, the outbreak of gunfire excited and incensed the white crowd. Hundreds of men, some of whom had been part of the mob just moments earlier, were deputized. A white man who was among those sworn in later said that the new deputies were told to "get a gun, get a nigger." In their fury at the armed Black men, the white mob largely forgot about Dick Rowland.[134]

Knots of angry white men prowled the streets of downtown Tulsa, looking for Black citizens to exact vengeance on. One unarmed Black man was chased by a group of white men through the streets and into a theater, where the pursuing mob caught up with him and killed him on stage.

The white throngs broke into hardware stores and pawn shops to steal guns and ammunition. Witnesses later testified that some uniformed Tulsa policemen participated in the break-ins and helped hand out firearms. Law officers and other government officials now became part of the mob and, along with the newly deputized would-be lynchers, lent it the color of authority.[135]

The armed Black men were driven across the Frisco tracks that separated Greenwood from downtown Tulsa shortly after midnight, but the outnumbered

Black men then made another determined stand. The two sides exchanged gunfire across and near the tracks for over an hour.[136]

After the Black defenders were finally forced to retreat, a few carloads of white men conducted drive-by shootings through the surrounding Black neighborhoods while others in the white mob began setting fires to Black homes. Initially, the Tulsa Fire Department responded to the fires to try to extinguish them, but the firemen were driven away at gunpoint by the white rioters. By 4:00 a.m. over two dozen homes and businesses in "Little Africa," as the white press disparagingly called the Black district, had been set ablaze.[137]

In the wee hours of Wednesday morning, the National Guard was called out, supposedly to restore and maintain order, but they spent most of their time protecting a white neighborhood from the nonexistent threat of a Black counterattack and rounding up Black civilians, whom they handed over to police as prisoners.[138]

In the predawn hours, thousands of armed white men gathered along the railroad tracks facing the Black district. With the coming of daylight, they poured across the tracks, backed by machine gun fire. The Black residents fought hard to defend the Greenwood Business District, but they were soon overwhelmed by the sheer number of invaders. National guardsmen traded gunfire with Black residents who had set up defensive lines on the edges of the Black neighborhood. Soon, several airplanes appeared in the sky, firing at Black residents and, in some cases, dropping incendiary devices.[139]

As more and more white rioters poured into the Black district and resistance softened, the attackers began systematically breaking into homes, looting them, driving out and arresting the occupants, and finally setting the homes on fire. Anyone who resisted was shot. The efforts of the Black residents who defended their neighborhood and their homes were hampered by Tulsa Police and the National Guard, who helped round up Black citizens and take them to temporary internment camps. In total, about six thousand Black Tulsans were interned.[140]

As the white mob moved north, they set fire to everything in their path, including churches, hotels, restaurants, stores, office buildings, and a Black public library. Some of the national guardsmen who had earlier exchanged fire with the Black defenders along the perimeter of the Greenwood District joined the rioters, marching through the district and firing at any Black residents who offered resistance.[141]

National guardsmen from Oklahoma City, or the state troops, as they were referred to in Tulsa, arrived around 9:15 a.m. on June 1. Most of the damage

The Black section of Tulsa burning during the Tulsa Race Riot. *Library of Congress*.

The Black section of Tulsa, or "Little Africa," as it was called at the time, burning during the Tulsa Race Riot. *Library of Congress*.

Furniture and other belongings piled in the street during the Tulsa Race Riot. *Library of Congress*.

had already been done, but the campaign of destruction continued while the state troops were trying to get organized or otherwise lollygagging. For instance, several homes of prominent Black citizens near Detroit Avenue and Easton Street that thus far had been spared were put to the torch by four Tulsa police officers who had been summoned to the scene to protect the homes.[142]

Martial law was finally declared around 11:30 a.m. Scattered pockets of white rioters continued to loot and burn for another hour, but most of them began to disperse. A final fight occurred around 12:30 p.m. near Pine Street and the railroad tracks when a group of Black defenders in a two-story building, who had held off the mob for hours, were finally driven from their stronghold, and the building was put to the torch.[143]

By this time, the state troops had begun occupying the Black neighborhoods and expelling white rioters. Some semblance of order was finally restored after more than fourteen hours of violence. Yet the ordeal for Black Tulsans was far from over. About ten thousand—almost the entire Black population of the city—were left homeless, with over half of them held in detention centers against their will.[144]

Sheriff McCullough secretly whisked Dick Rowland out of town sometime during the riot. Sarah Page later declined to prosecute, and Rowland was exonerated. But even today, Tulsa is reckoning with a legacy of racial hatred that has stained the city for over a hundred years because of the senseless violence sparked by a casual encounter between the two young people.[145]

In the immediate aftermath of the Tulsa riot, white newspapers put the blame for the violence squarely on the Black community, specifically the Black men who'd arrived at the courthouse to offer their help to protect Dick Rowland. The *Tulsa Tribune* claimed, for instance, that a mostly unarmed white crowd had gathered at the courthouse simply "out of curiosity" and that the situation became violent only because the armed Black men showed up and paraded back and forth, "muttering threats and brandishing their firearms," and generally appeared "overly anxious for an encounter."[146]

Other white Tulsans agreed. Two weeks after the riot, the Tulsa City Commission issued a report that said, in part, "Let the blame for this negro uprising lie right where it belongs—on those armed negros and their followers who started this trouble." An all-white grand jury that was impaneled to investigate the riot and prosecute wrongdoers concluded that the riot was the direct result of "a certain group of colored men" appearing at the courthouse on the night of May 31. The white men assembled at the courthouse, said the jury, were purely spectators and curiosity-seekers who'd gathered peaceably and evinced no mob spirit and no intent to carry out a lynching. The jury did indict eighty-five people, but they were mostly Black, and few, if any, of the indictments resulted in prosecution.[147]

For many years after the Tulsa Race Massacre, or "race riot," as it was usually called, the event was rarely talked about, especially in Tulsa, and

Left: The west side of Greenwood Street, in the heart of Tulsa's Black district, after the riot. *Library of Congress*.

Following: Tulsa's "Burnt District" after the race riot. *Library of Congress*.

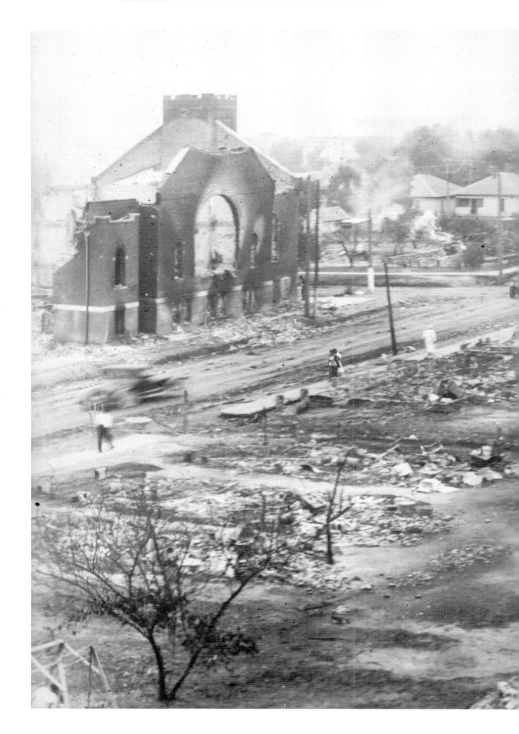

the subject was not included in history books to teach schoolchildren about it in Oklahoma.[148]

Although thousands of Black Americans were displaced by the 1921 riot, Tulsa's Black community almost immediately began rebuilding with little to no help from the white members of the community. By the 1940s, the Greenwood District had once again grown into a prospering business area, but urban renewal and efforts at integration led to decline in the 1960s and 1970s.[149]

The State of Oklahoma formed a commission in 1997 to study and document the 1921 Tulsa Race Massacre. Members of the committee interviewed survivors of the tragedy, gathered eyewitness accounts from people who have since died, and examined other pieces of historical evidence. Using witness accounts and ground-penetrating radar, scientists and scholars located potential grave sites that suggested the number of people killed during the massacre might far exceed original estimates.[150]

The commission's report recommended that reparations be paid to the remaining Black survivors, who numbered about 120. No legislative action was ever taken on the recommendation, although a private religious charity in Tulsa did distribute about $28,000 to survivors in 2002.[151]

8

THE OSAGE MURDERS

A DIABOLICAL SCHEME

On May 27, 1921, the body of Anna Brown was found beside a road between Fairfax and Grayhorse in Osage County, Oklahoma. The thirty-four-year-old Brown had been shot through the head, and she had been dead for several days. Initial reports mentioned that Brown was separated (i.e., divorced) from her white husband; that, as a member of the Osage tribe, she was receiving about $1,000 per month in "oil royalties"; and that her white guardian was a man named B.F. Mason. However, the only theory of the crime local authorities could offer was that she had been the victim of highway robbery, since several valuable rings were missing from her fingers.[152]

As it turned out, Anna Brown was the victim not of an ordinary highway robbery but of one of the most diabolical get-rich schemes in American history.

The background behind that get-rich scheme goes back to the late 1800s, when the Osage Nation was forced off its lands in Kansas. With the blessing of the federal government, the tribe purchased land in Northeast Oklahoma. The tribe held the land collectively at first, but the Dawes Act was enacted in 1887 to parcel out Native land to individuals. The rocky, barren Osage land was considered virtually worthless until one of the largest deposits of oil in the United States was discovered beneath its surface in the 1890s. And when a statute was finally passed in 1906 that allotted Osage land as called for by the Dawes Act, the Osage shrewdly negotiated two important provisions to help them retain their newfound wealth: only members of the Osage tribe could receive allotments and the rights to mineral resources like coal and oil would be owned collectively by the tribe, regardless of who owned the land.[153]

To divide up the profits from the commonly owned mineral rights, a system was adopted by which each Osage member on the tribal rolls in 1907 would receive an equal share of the revenue. This came to be called a headright. Private companies could lease the land from the tribe in order to extract oil, coal, and other minerals, and they would pay a percentage of their profits into a trust fund managed by the Bureau of Indian Affairs (BIA). The BIA would then distribute payments to the holders of the headrights.[154]

Anna Brown. *Courtesy of the FBI.*

During the Oklahoma oil boom of the early 1900s, the Osage people became some of the wealthiest in the world. Members of the tribe, like Anna Brown, received payments that, adjusted for inflation, would today be worth hundreds of thousands of dollars per year. Many Osages purchased large homes, fancy clothes, and expensive cars.[155]

The sudden wealth of the Osage people drew lots of swindlers looking to cheat tribal members out of their money, so the U.S. government established a system that was supposedly designed to help the Osage protect their wealth. White guardians were assigned to manage the money of any member of the tribe who was judged to be incompetent. In practice, however, the guardianship program was a racist system under which simply being Native was a sufficient reason to be deemed "incompetent."[156]

Guardians often paid themselves using the money they were supposed to be safeguarding, and they would give their Osage wards only small allowances. This, however, was not the worst of the abuses. The Osage Allotment Act provided that headrights could not be sold but could be inherited. This inheritance provision spawned what came to be known as the "Osage Reign of Terror," during which many white people married into the Osage tribe and then killed or hired someone else to kill their spouses and/or their spouse's relatives in order to gain their headrights.[157]

Anna Brown was not the first victim of the scheme. In retrospect, even the death of her sister Minnie in 1918 from what was labeled "wasting illness" seems suspicious. However, most of the murders of Osage people occurred during the "Reign of Terror" of the early 1920s, and Anna's killing was one of the first that was widely reported. At least twenty-four members of the Osage tribe were killed or died under mysterious circumstances during this period, and some estimates place the number of victims at more than twice that figure. Most of the murders occurred in the Fairfax-Grayhorse area, and many of the victims were members of the same family, relatives of Anna Brown.[158]

On May 27, 1921, the same day Anna's body was found, the body of her cousin Charles Whitehorn was found in a different part of the county, near Pawhuska. He had been shot twice in the head and had been dead for several days. A coroner's jury ruled a few days later that he had come to his death at the hands of parties unknown.[159]

The investigation into Anna's death took longer. Several people were arrested for questioning or as suspects in the crime, including brothers Bryan and Ernest Burkhart, the latter of whom was married to Anna's sister Mollie. However, the coroner's jury in Anna's case ultimately reached the same conclusion that the Whitehorn jury had reached.[160]

On July 17, less than two months after Anna was killed, her mother, Lizzie Q. Kyle (also known as Lizzie Que), died at her home in Grayhorse. Her death was scarcely noted by the press. The local newspaper mentioned only that Lizzie was the mother of Mrs. William E. "Rita" Smith and Mollie Burkhart of Grayhorse. At the time of her death, Lizzie owned at least three full headrights. In addition to her own, she had inherited headrights from her deceased husband and her deceased daughter, Minnie. Now, she was in line to inherit Anna's headright as well. Lizzie's son-in-law Bill Smith suspected that Lizzie had been poisoned, but no serious investigation into her death was undertaken. Smith and others began to believe that something evil was afoot.[161]

On February 6, 1923, Henry Roan, to whom Anna Brown had once been briefly married, was found dead in his car in a ravine about four miles north of Fairfax. He had been shot in the back of the head and had been dead for several days.[162]

Just a month later, in the wee hours of the morning on March 10, a terrific explosion blew up the Fairfax home of Bill and Rita Smith, instantly killing Rita and the couple's live-in maid, Nettie Brookshire. Bill Smith died a couple of days later from injuries he sustained in the explosion and resultant fire. He said on his deathbed that he had only two enemies in world: Ernest Burkhart and Bill Hale, who was Ernest's uncle.[163]

 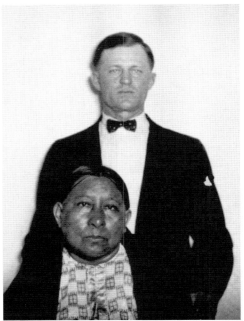

Left: Rita Smith (*left*) with her servant, Nettie Brookshire. *Courtesy of the FBI.*

Right: Ernest and Mollie Burkhart. *Oklahoma Historical Society*.

The coincidence of so many members of the Osage tribe, especially members of the same family, dying so close together was becoming too obvious to ignore. According to newspaper reports about the explosion, authorities believed there might have been a connection between it and the murder of Mrs. Smith's sister, Anna Brown, near Fairfax two years earlier. There was speculation that Bill Smith was targeted because he was trying to have Anna's death investigated. The people of Fairfax were "badly wrought up" over the latest incident, and they were planning to ask the Osage Council to initiate an investigation into the matter. Still, there were no serious suspects identified and no charges brought in the immediate aftermath of the explosion.[164]

Even those who tried to investigate the mysterious Osage deaths had a tendency to turn up dead. For instance, in late June 1923, George Bigheart, a wealthy Osage from Fairfax, got sick after ingesting poisoned whiskey and was taken to an Oklahoma City hospital. Bigheart summoned lawyer W.W. Vaughan to the hospital from Pawhuska for an urgent meeting because he had information about the Osage murders. The two conferred upon Vaughan's arrival, and Bigheart died shortly afterward. Late on the night of June 29, Vaughan boarded a train headed back to Pawhuska. When he did not arrive at his destination on schedule, a search was undertaken, and his body was found on July 1 on the tracks about fifty miles outside Oklahoma City. Investigators concluded that he had simply fallen from the vestibule of the train.[165]

The Osage Council did initiate an investigation into the mysterious deaths of so many members of its tribe, but it got very little cooperation from local and state authorities. The Osage leaders then appealed to the federal government, which sent agents of the Bureau of Investigation (the forerunner of the Federal Bureau of Investigation, or FBI) to look into the spate of Osage murders.[166]

The bureau's investigation stalled until Tom White, a former Texas Ranger, took over the probe in 1925. The investigative team kept encountering the names of William K. Hale, Ernest Burkhart, and local bootlegger John Ramsey. The first two, of course, were the very men Bill Smith had named on his deathbed as his enemies. Under intense questioning, Burkhart implicated Ramsey in the killing of Henry Roan, and Ramsey, in turn, said that Hale, who was the beneficiary of Roan's life insurance policy, had hired him to do the deed.[167]

John Ramsey also admitted his involvement in the Smith explosion and named Hale as the mastermind of that crime as well. Hale, the so-called King of the Osage Hills, was a wealthy, prominent citizen of the Fairfax

William Hale, the ringleader behind the Osage murders. *Courtesy of the FBI.*

area who posed as a friend of the Natives. In truth, he was conspiring with his nephew Ernest Burkhart to kill the family members of Ernest's wife, Mollie, so that the two men could inherit the family's headrights.[168]

At the time the conspiracy was uncovered, Mollie Burkhart was very sick. Agents thought she was being slowly poisoned by her doctors, who were in cahoots with her husband and Hale. She, like her sisters, probably would have died had the investigation dragged on much longer, but she recovered quickly once she was removed from her doctors' care.[169]

On January 4, 1926, Hale and Ernest Burkhart were indicted for the murders of the Smiths, and a few days later, Hale

William Hale and John Ramsey flanked by law officers. *Oklahoma Historical Society.*

and Ramsey were charged in the Roan murder. Later in the year, Bryan Burkhart, one of the early suspects in the Anna Brown case, was rearrested for her murder and charged jointly with local ne'er-do-well Kelsie Morrison, who was already in prison for a different crime.[170]

The defendants were tried in state and federal courts over a period of more than three years. Ernest Burkhart pleaded guilty in June 1926 to the murder of William Smith and was sentenced to life imprisonment in the Oklahoma State Penitentiary. He later testified against Hale and Ramsey in the Henry Roan murder case. Both defendants in that case were found guilty and sentenced in 1929 to life imprisonment in the Leavenworth Federal Penitentiary. Morrison was found guilty of the Anna Brown murder and sentenced to life imprisonment, while Bryan Burkhart, who turned state's evidence, was not prosecuted for the crime.[171]

All the central figures in the Osage murders were eventually paroled, despite protests from the Osage Nation. Hale was paroled in 1947 after serving only eighteen years. Burkhart and Ramsey were also released early, and Burkhart eventually received a full pardon in 1965.[172]

Although the mysterious deaths in Mollie Burkhart's family were the focus of Tom White's investigation, there were many other murders and unexplained deaths of Osage tribal members during the Reign of Terror. To prevent another such outrage, the U.S. Congress passed a law in 1925 barring non-Osages from inheriting the headrights of tribal members who were more than one-half Osage by blood.[173]

The Osage murders of the early twentieth century were the subjects of David Grann's 2017 book, *Killers of the Flower Moon*, and a popular movie of the same name, based on the book and directed by Martin Scorsese, was released in 2023.

9
THE SEVERS HOTEL MURDERS

A round 8:30 p.m. on Saturday, April 26, 1930, the telephone operator at the elegant Severs Hotel in Muskogee received a frantic call from a guest in room 817 who said that his friends had been robbed and killed. The operator relayed the message to the assistant hotel manager Lee Jones, who dismissed the call as some sort of prank. The same person immediately called again and urgently pleaded for help, so Jones called police. He then hurried to the eighth floor to investigate. Still thinking the call might be a prank, Jones peeked through the keyhole of room 817 and saw a man with a red mark on his face talking to another man. The red mark looked like blood. Jones went back downstairs to get hotel engineer Barney Sullivan, and the two men returned to room 817 to find the door locked. Someone inside the room tried to open the door but could not, and Jones also could not open it when he tried using his pass key. Sullivan then opened the door with his key. He and Jones found an elderly man in the room with shaving cream on his face, a second man lying on the floor nearby with his hands bound, and two other men lying lifelessly on the floor across the room, near the door of adjoining room 819.[174]

The man with his hands bound and the elderly man identified themselves as John L. Wike and P.G. Seeley, respectively, and the two dead men were brothers David and George Smith. The four men had traveled together on business from Connecticut. Wike said that two men had forced their way into the adjoining room and attacked the Smith brothers.[175]

HOTEL SEVERS.   MUSKOGEE, OKLA.

The Hotel Severs around the time of the Smith murders. *Three Rivers Museum of Muskogee Collection.*

CONNECTICUT MEN HELD AT MUSKOGEE

Murder Charges Filed Against Two Men From Native State Of Victims

---

Headline announcing the arrest of Wike and Seeley. *From the* Vinita Daily Journal.

Wike said he wanted to leave his hands bound until police arrived so that authorities could see the crime scene undisturbed. Detective Ted Conway untied him when he and Detective Jess Adair arrived a few minutes later. Wike then explained again what had happened, repeating in more detail what he'd told Jones and Sullivan.[176]

All four men were associated with the bankrupt New Milford Security Company of Connecticut, and they had traveled to Oklahoma together to check on the status of mortgages the company held on certain western lands. They had spent Friday night in Springfield, Missouri, and then motored to Muskogee on Saturday, arriving in the late afternoon. After checking into the Severs Hotel, they ate dinner at a nearby café and then met with V.R. Coss, a local representative of the New Milford company.[177]

According to Wike's story, the four men returned to their hotel suite around 8:00 p.m. The seventy-three-year-old Seeley retired to the bathroom of room 817 to shave, while the other three men, who were all about middle aged, continued discussing business in the adjoining room, 819, where the Smith brothers were staying. David Smith was seated on the bed, and George Smith and Wike were sitting at a table across the room when, suddenly, two men burst into the room unannounced.[178]

David Smith asked what they wanted, and one of the two flourished a pistol and said, "We'll show you what we want."

David Smith jumped from the bed and wrapped his arms around the gunman. When the second intruder moved to help his partner, George Smith sprang up and threw himself on the second man.[179]

Relating Wike's version of story two days later, the *Muskogee Daily Phoenix* said,

The room immediately became the scene of a furious struggle, with the two pair of combatants whirling around each other, fighting desperately for an advantage.

Wike was penned in one corner when he saw David Smith, who was a large, powerful man, bend his antagonist over; Wike then grabbed the bandit by one foot and lifted it off the floor, only to find himself hurtled through the air, just before he crashed head-on against a wall, he told police.

Wike thought he was thrown into the wall when David Smith swung his assailant in a wide arc to keep the man from pressing a pistol to his body.[180]

Meanwhile, George Smith and the second intruder struggled into the adjoining room, and Wike almost immediately heard the "rapid staccato sound of four shots." The first shot did not take effect, but the second struck George Smith in the lower abdomen, the third hit him in the pit of his stomach, and the fourth bored straight into his heart.

David Smith was shot through the mouth, with the bullet ranging downward into one of his lungs. The same weapon killed both brothers, but investigators did not know for sure whether the man who had killed George Smith also killed David Smith or, instead, handed the gun to his partner, who killed the latter Smith.[181]

After killing both Smiths, the bandits jerked Wike from the room where the fight started into the other room, made him get on the floor, and bound and gagged him. They quickly rifled through his pockets but took only his wallet from a hip pocket, even though some of his other pockets contained money and valuables.[182]

Seeley told the police he was in the bathroom when the intrusion occurred and did not hear any sounds of a struggle or argument, but he did hear four shots. Wike said he knew of nobody who might have committed the crime, and he thought robbery was the only motive.

Police tentatively accepted that theory but grew skeptical as they began investigating the crime. The first question that arose was the mystery of why, if robbery were the motive, the bandits took only a small portion of the money and valuables the four men had in their possession. As a Muskogee newspaper phrased it: Why did the robbers take time to bind and gag Wike but "did not take sufficient time to loot the baggage of any of the men, and made a very cursory examination of the men's pockets"? The newspaper wondered why the robbers took a small ring from George Smith's hand but did not bother with the money in his pockets. Nor did

DAVID F. SMITH.   GEORGE R. SMITH.

Newspaper photograph of murder victims David and George Smith. *From the* Hartford (CT) Courant.

they take the money that was in the pocket of his brother's coat, which was hanging in the closet. Yet they took about $300 in traveler's checks, which were worthless unless countersigned.[183]

Not convinced by the story that Wike and Seeley told, police grilled the two men all day Sunday and into the night. Officers wanted to know why Seeley did not hear the commotion in the next room from where he was shaving and why he did not untie Wike immediately upon discovering him bound and gagged. If there was a terrific struggle prior to the firing of shots, as Wike maintained, why was the room relatively undisturbed, why were George Smith's spectacles still in place on his nose when his body was found, and why were his necktie and that of his brother still perfectly arranged? Why did Wike lie so passively on the floor with his hands tied while Seeley called for help and while waiting for the help to arrive, given the fact that his feet were not bound and he could have gotten up at any time. And why did Seeley not untie Wike when he first discovered him bound and gagged on the floor?[184]

TWO CLEARED OF MURDER CHARGES

John L. Wike (left) and Powell G. Seeley, both of Connecticut,

Sketch of murder suspects John Wike (*left*) and P.G. Seeley. *From the* Muskogee Daily Phoenix.

Seeley calmly explained that he was hard of hearing and that, even when he heard the gunshots, he wasn't sure what they were or that they had come from the adjoining room. Wike said the reason he was still bound when help arrived was that he wanted authorities to see the scene exactly as it appeared after the crime was committed.[185]

Calls to Connecticut confirmed that the four men from that state were prominent and trustworthy citizens who'd never been in trouble with the law. Arguing in their favor, also, was the fact that neither the murder weapon nor the room key had been found. If Wike and Seeley had murdered the Smith brothers, how did they dispose of those items? The only windows in their room faced a well-lighted, main street. It seemed unlikely they could have thrown the gun and the key out the windows without being seen or without someone finding the items, and a thorough search of the two rooms did not turn up the items.[186]

Most of the lawmen involved in investigating the case soon came to believe that Wike and Seeley were not implicated in the murders. The pair was released around noon on Monday under the stipulation that they not leave Muskogee and that they thoroughly cooperate with the officers in their investigation.[187]

Authorities now felt that the motive for the crime likely had something to do with the foursome's association with the New Milford Security Company. Perhaps a mortgage holder who blamed the company for his financial ruin killed the brothers in an act of revenge. If this was the case, however, why did such a person not attack the brothers somewhere on the road before they were ensconced in their hotel room? Because of all the unanswered questions surrounding the case, many observers felt, as the *Muskogee Daily Phoenix* said, that the slayers of the Smith brothers were "now hiding safely behind a fog of mysteries that may never be penetrated."[188]

Later on Monday, officers searched Seeley's luggage after the two men were moved to the Baltimore Hotel at their own request. The officers found a diamond ring that Wike had previously reported had been taken from George Smith's hand by the killers. It had not been in Seeley's luggage when officers initially searched it on Saturday night right after the murders. Seeley swore he knew nothing about the ring or how it had gotten there. About the same time, an unexplained bloodstain was discovered on the back of Wike's coat. He and Seeley were rearrested, charged with murder, and closely guarded at the hotel. The general feeling was still that Wike and Seeley were not guilty, but assistant prosecutor Phil Oldham felt that indicting the two would expedite the investigation.[189]

The suspects remained calm through several more hours of questioning. Seeley was so jovial that one reporter remarked that not only did he believe the man was innocent, but he also could hardly believe that a murder had been committed. Although Seeley remained cheerful, he thought it ridiculous that he and Wike were suspected of killing their friends. He deeply regretted that they had not been allowed to accompany the bodies of the Smith brothers back to Connecticut.[190]

Remarking on the disarming personalities of the two suspects, one officer complained that, although the circumstances suggested they were somehow involved in the crime, when he talked to them, he found it "almost impossible to even suggest to them that you think they might have done it."[191]

A preliminary hearing for the two men was held on May 1 in the district courtroom at Muskogee before an overflow crowd. Prosecutor Oldham focused much of his attention on the fact that the missing ring was found in Seeley's luggage, but he had little solid evidence to present. The defense, on the other hand, suggested that some "suspicious characters" who had been seen loitering around the hotel shortly before the murders might well have committed the crime. Wike and Seeley's lawyer also emphasized their unblemished records and outstanding reputations back home in Connecticut. The tide turned in the defense's favor when Sheriff Fred Hamilton, who'd interviewed the suspects multiple times, took the stand and stated emphatically that he felt the defendants were not guilty. All doubt about the outcome of the hearing was erased when Wike and Seeley, when testifying in their own defense, calmly told their stories very much like they had told them from the outset. By the end of the hearing, even Oldham had been won over. In his closing argument, he shot holes in his own evidence and admitted that there was not enough probable cause to hold the two men. When the judge announced that the charges against the Connecticut men were dismissed, the courtroom erupted into applause.[192]

Wike and Seeley were allowed to go back to Connecticut under bond to appear as material witnesses if and when developments in the double-murder case warranted their return. The crime gradually receded from the spotlight, and the investigation into the murders stalled. Numerous leads of mysterious men seen lurking around the Severs Hotel or the hotel in Springfield, Missouri, where the foursome had spent the night prior to the murders, were checked, but none led anywhere. In mid-May, interest in the case was revived when some papers belonging to David Smith were found on a Muskogee street, but that lead, too, proved fruitless. When a missing hotel key from the third floor of the Severs was found in rural Muskogee County later the same month, some investigators, grasping at straws, tried to read significance into that discovery as well but to no avail.[193]

A break in the Severs Hotel case came in early June, when R.L. Benton, an alleged member of a holdup gang that was known to be in the Muskogee vicinity on the night of the murders, was arrested in Miami, Oklahoma, in connection with a series of robberies in southwest Missouri and northeast Oklahoma. In mid-June, Wike journeyed back to Oklahoma from Connecticut and identified Benton as one of the men who had attacked and killed the Smith brothers. Held on charges of robbery and suspicion of murder at the Muskogee County Jail, Benton escaped in early August.[194]

In mid-November, a gunman shot and killed a police officer in Kirksville, Missouri, when the officer stopped him for questioning. The killer was later identified as veteran criminal Lawrence Devol (alias R.L. Benton), the same man wanted in connection with the Smith murders. A large manhunt for Devol, a known associate of notorious criminals like Harvey Bailey and Alvin Karpis, was launched throughout the Midwest, but nothing was heard from Devol until about a year later, when he joined the infamous Barker gang. In late 1932, Devol killed two policemen outside a Minnesota bank during the gang's robbery of the place. Devol was captured, convicted of murder, and sentenced to life imprisonment. He escaped from a hospital for the criminally insane in June 1936. Later the same month, he and a companion, Albert "Scarface" Soroko, tried to hold up a café in Oklahoma City, and Soroko was killed in a police shootout. The following month, Devol killed a policeman and seriously wounded a second in Enid, Oklahoma, when the two officers tried to question him. Devol was then killed in a second gun battle with police just moments later.[195]

Gangster Jimmy Creighton was eventually identified as the other prime suspect aside from Devol in the Severs Hotel murders, but he was already serving a life sentence in the Missouri penitentiary. Since no one was ever tried or convicted for the murders of David and George Smith, the crime officially remains an unsolved mystery.[196]

THE MANHUNT FOR PRETTY BOY FLOYD

n early 1934, the Cookson Hills of eastern Oklahoma carried a notorious reputation as a haven for criminals. As one Oklahoma City newspaperman phrased it at the time, "Outlaws since the days of Judge Isaac C. Parker, Fort Smith, Ark., hanging jurist of pioneer days, have fled to the dense woods of the hills as a refuge."[197]

National publicity surrounding the recent exploits of Charles "Pretty Boy" Floyd and the 1933 kidnapping of wealthy Oklahoma City resident Charles Urschel by George "Machine Gun" Kelly had added another "black mark" to Oklahoma's reputation. Eager to vindicate the state's name, Oklahoma government and law enforcement officials planned a massive dragnet of the Cookson Hills. They were merely waiting for Floyd, who'd grown up in those hills, to return to his old haunts before putting their plan into action.[198]

Charles Arthur Floyd was born in Georgia in 1904 and moved with his family to eastern Oklahoma when he was about seven years old. He left home when he was sixteen and became involved in bootlegging and other illegal activities while he was still a teenager. His first serious trouble with the law came in 1925, when he and two companions robbed a Kroger store in St. Louis of about $12,000 in payroll. The caper earned Floyd a five-year sentence in the Missouri State Penitentiary.[199]

Upon his release in 1929, Floyd headed to Kansas City. There, he met a future girlfriend, who gave him the nickname "Pretty Boy," and he quickly embarked on a string of bank robberies that would continue until his death. He was implicated in several other crimes that he did not commit. While earning a notorious reputation among law enforcement that eventually led to his being named public enemy no. 1, Floyd was elevated at the same time by many poor people during the Depression era to the status of folk hero, a sort of glorified Robin Hood figure who was on the side of the common man. He was immortalized in a Woody Guthrie song and in John Steinback's *Grapes of Wrath*.[200]

On April 7, 1932, Erv Kelley, the ex-sheriff of McIntosh County turned bounty hunter, passed through Muskogee on the trail of Pretty Boy Floyd. The outlaw's former wife had recently returned from Tulsa to stay with her father, Ben Hardgrave, near Bixby, and Kelley had received information that Floyd would likely show up at his ex-father-in-law's house to visit his ex-wife and son. Kelley told Muskogee chief of police John Wolsey, "I have a date with Floyd."[201]

Kelley and a posse of seven other men staked out Floyd's father-in-law's home on the night of April 8. After waiting in vain for several hours for Floyd to appear, Kelley decided that he'd received faulty intelligence, and he called off the vigil at about 2:30 a.m. on April 9. He told the other posse members to go back to Bixby to get their car, which they'd left there so that they could approach the Hardgrave home undetected. Meanwhile, Kelley, still armed with a machine gun, went to the nearby home of Cecil Bennett to tell two farmers who'd been stationed there as a precaution that the stakeout was over.[202]

Kelley was talking to the two farmers at a chicken house located on a lane between the main road and the Bennett farmhouse when a car turned into the lane. Not recognizing the vehicle, Kelley ordered the driver to halt. The driver and his passenger (who proved to be Pretty Boy Floyd and his partner Earl Birdwell) answered the command with a burst of .45-caliber gunfire that mowed Kelley down. The desperadoes then wheeled their car around, sped away to the southwest, and outdistanced a police pursuit.[203]

One of Floyd's most celebrated bank heists came later in the year when he held up the Sallisaw State Bank in his hometown of Sallisaw. Shortly before noon on November 1, 1932, Floyd and Birdwell strode into the bank while a third member of the gang waited in a nearby getaway car. Pulling a revolver and a submachine gun from beneath their coats, Floyd and Birdwell ordered cashier Bob Riggs and two customers to "stick 'em up." Floyd rifled the tills and cleaned out the safe while Birdwell kept the hostages covered with the submachine gun. Riggs recognized Floyd, and the two carried on a conversation during the holdup. Floyd told Riggs and the other hostages that if they would "be careful and not make any disturbance…nobody would get hurt."[204]

More customers entered the bank while the robbery was taking place, and Birdwell herded a few passersby inside as well to prevent them from sounding an alarm. As the holdup neared its end, about a dozen hostages were corralled inside the bank. After the holdup men had taken nearly every penny in the bank, estimated between $5,000 and $6,000, they forced Riggs to accompany them outside and herded him into the getaway car. They let him out unharmed just outside town and sped toward Arkansas, eluding officers who gave chase.[205]

Interviewed after the robbery, Riggs said he was sure of Floyd's identity. "We know Chuck over here. He grew up just a little piece from town. He recognized several of the customers who came in during the robbery." Riggs said Floyd and his companion stayed calm throughout the holdup and "treated their acquaintances with consideration and respect."[206]

In June 1933, Floyd became a prime suspect in the so-called Kansas City Massacre, in which four law officers were slain at Union Station. The notoriety surrounding the infamous slaughter eventually propelled Floyd to the status of public enemy no. 1, even though some historians now claim that Floyd was not involved in the incident.[207]

In mid-February 1934, Oklahoma authorities received the intelligence they had been waiting for as a signal to begin their massive sweep of the Cookson Hills. Charles "Pretty Boy" Floyd was reported to be back in Oklahoma. On Friday, February 16, Floyd and a companion picked up three Weatherford High School girls as they were walking into town. According to the girls, Floyd asked them if they knew who he was, and when one of them recognized him, she gasped, "You're Pretty Boy Floyd." He acknowledged that he was indeed the noted gangster, and he showed the girls a cache of weapons, including several machine guns. Floyd offered to drive the girls to the local police station if they wanted to turn him in and collect a couple of thousand dollars in reward money, but they declined the offer. He then let them out unharmed on Weatherford's main street.[208]

At 4:00 p.m. the next day, what was described at the time as "the nation's biggest manhunt" was launched in eastern Oklahoma, covering four hundred square miles of the rugged Cookson Hills. A force of about one thousand men, including U.S. agents, state officers, county sheriffs, and police officers from the main towns in the area, swept into the hills from four different

Charles "Pretty Boy" Floyd. *Courtesy of the FBI.*

directions. Headquarters to coordinate the operation were established in four towns: Muskogee, Stilwell, Tahlequah, and Sallisaw. Police officers in western Arkansas were also cooperating in the massive raid. The huge posse had orders to patrol highways, search residences, and scour the woods and ravines of the "most notorious rendezvous of criminals in the Southwest." Their biggest target was the elusive Pretty Boy Floyd.[209]

Late on Saturday evening, Oklahoma governor W.H. Murray called out the National Guard in the eastern part of the state to join the search. Armed with regulation rifles and sidearms, a total of about three hundred guardsmen were eventually ordered out from Tahlequah, Wagoner, and Muskogee. Led by military officers and veteran lawmen, the guardsmen began a march "through the wilderness of hills, timber, and gullies from Muskogee to Stilwell." This area, according to *Oklahoma City News* reporter Noel Houston, was considered the "very heart of the worst of the section."[210]

Even prison guards from the state penitentiary at McAlester reinforced the large search party.

The searchers had orders to "arrest if possible, kill if necessary." Houston, the *News* reporter, described the disposition of these forces on Saturday night:

> *Rifles, riot guns, pistols and machine guns bristled on every corner of the key towns and on every highway held in the hands of officers who were ready to shoot any known bandit or murderer who attempted to break through the cordon.*
>
> *Arkansas officers moved in from Siloam Springs....Peace officers from the Vinita section covered the northern front.*[211]

Roadblocks were set up, and every vehicle that entered or left the Cookson Hills "war zone" was stopped. The occupants were questioned, and the vehicles were searched. "Suspicious persons" were arrested and taken to one of the headquarter towns for fingerprinting. They were jailed pending the results of the prints.

The Illinois River flows through the Cookson Hills, and the Arkansas River borders the hills on the south. "The countless canyons and caves" along their banks "have hidden criminals from pioneer days," Houston told his readers. "The Kimes brothers, Al Jennings gang, the Doolins and Daltons have sought shelter in the almost inaccessible ravines."[212]

The reporter called the drive through the hills by the army of law enforcement officers "the most sensational organized war on crime ever staged in Oklahoma and perhaps the largest manhunt ever staged in the nation."[213]

After accompanying a posse led by Oklahoma County sheriff Stanley Rogers in its push through the Cookson Hills on Saturday evening and during the day on Sunday, Houston reported on Monday that the mammoth manhunt had largely been a failure and that the officers composing it had begun to demobilize. "The Cookson Hills are still impenetrable," he said. "It will take more than 500 officers or 1,000 officers and militiamen or however many of us there were patroling the highways from Muskogee to Stilwell, from Sallisaw to Tahlequah, to trap the gang of criminals lurking in those jumbled timbered hills."[214]

The reporter explained that the gigantic dragnet had caught a few "minnows" but that the big fish like Pretty Boy Floyd were nowhere to be seen. "I never realized," Houston continued, "the full significance of the newspaper phrase 'The bandits escaped into the Cookson Hills and the officers turned back' until I toured those blue, oak-strewn hills Sunday with Sheriff Stanley Rogers."[215]

The problem, Houston said, was that although the hills seemed calm, the officers knew that, in all likelihood, "on the other side of every hill that [they] passed…an outlaw who would kill [them] at the slightest excuse lay in hiding." Houston said he himself had "an uncomfortable, humiliating feeling that every hill we passed shielded an outlaw peering down on us who laughed to himself."[216]

At many of the houses the officers checked, they found nobody at home. If they did find someone, that person was usually someone whose worst crime might be possession of a little illegal whiskey. The officers suspected that the occupants of the vacated houses had simply retreated into the dense woods. However, to try to ferret out all the men who were willing to kill on sight from their hiding places would have meant certain death for many of the posse members. The only practical plan was to nab such desperate characters if and when they tried to get past one of the roadblocks, but very few made such an attempt.[217]

The huge sweep through the Cookson Hills had been planned under the assumption that the outlaws would do one of two things: either they would try to escape via the highways and run into a police blockade, or they would hole up in their homes. They did neither.[218]

The closest the manhunt came to netting a big fish occurred when a car carrying a driver, a male companion, and a woman failed to stop for a roadblock about four miles west of Sallisaw. The vehicle ran "a gauntlet of gunfire" and was "peppered with bullets" as it made its escape. The driver of the auto was thought to be Clyde Barrow, and his woman companion was believed to be "Bonnie Parker, Dallas cigar smoking schoolgirl companion of Barrow."[219]

Houston, the *News* reporter, claimed that the manhunt's meager catch was not the fault of the officers. They worked hard and were eager to catch outlaws, but they had been foiled by nature. "It was not the outlaws who outwitted the officers," Houston concluded. "The Cookson Hills are a fortress which an army of 500 or 1,000 cannot capture."[220]

Although Floyd managed to escape law enforcement's huge dragnet of the Cookson Hills—if, indeed, he ever was there at the time of the operation—his date with destiny loomed in the near future. On October 22, 1934, Pretty Boy was gunned down by FBI agents and local lawmen in a field near East Liverpool, Ohio. His body was brought back to Oklahoma for burial in the Akins Cemetery. An estimated crowd of over twenty thousand people attended the burial, making it the largest funeral in state history.[221]

11

BONNIE AND CLYDE AND THE MURDER OF COMMERCE CONSTABLE CAL CAMPBELL

Most students of regional or gangster history are well acquainted with Bonnie and Clyde's April 1933 shootout with police in Joplin, Missouri, which left two officers dead, but the Barrow gang's murder of one law officer and wounding and kidnapping of another just across the border from Joplin in Commerce, Oklahoma, a year later has received less publicity and notoriety, even though it was almost equally horrific.

Around 9:30 a.m. on Friday, April 6, 1934, a motorist reported to Commerce constable Cal Campbell that he had just passed a car at the side of a road on the southwest edge of town containing two men and a woman whom he considered suspicious-looking characters. When Campbell and Police Chief Percy Boyd arrived on the scene, the driver of the suspect vehicle, later identified as Clyde Barrow, rammed his car into reverse and started back down the road "wide open," but the automobile, a new Ford V-8, veered into a ditch and got stuck in the mud.[222]

Campbell and Boyd got out of their car and started walking toward the stranded vehicle. When Campbell noticed that the occupants of the suspect car were brandishing weapons, he drew his pistol and opened fire. Someone in the car responded by firing two shots from a shotgun, and then Barrow and another man leaped out of the stranded Ford carrying automatic rifles and started running toward the lawmen, firing as they came.[223]

Campbell got off three shots before he was killed in the hail of bullets. Boyd, who managed to fire his weapon four times, was also knocked off his feet but received only a flesh wound. He later estimated that the gangsters must have fired eighty shots at him and his partner.[224]

After the shooting stopped, Barrow ran toward a nearby farmhouse, while the other man walked toward Boyd and ordered him to get up. The chief made a joke as he got to his feet, which seemed to put the gunman "in a good humor."[225]

Barrow and his sidekicks tried to pull their stuck vehicle out of the mud with a pickup truck, which was commandeered either from the farmhouse or a passing motorist. Unable to get the Ford out of the ditch, they ordered Boyd to help them, and they forced three other men who appeared on the scene to help as well. When a concerted effort still wouldn't budge the mired vehicle, Barrow threatened to kill the four men if they couldn't get the car unstuck.[226]

The gang was about ready to steal a car that was parked in a nearby yard when C.M. Dodson, who'd heard the gunfire, arrived in a truck to investigate the sounds. Barrow and his male companion ordered Dodson to pull their car out of the hole with a chain he had in the truck. One of the men held a gun on Dodson and the other bystanders while the chain was tied around the Ford, and then Dodson got back into his truck and pulled the car out of the ditch.[227]

As soon as the truck driver pulled the stranded vehicle out of the ditch, he noticed Boyd being led around the car and forced into the backseat with blood streaming down his face. He also saw a young woman, later identified as Bonnie Parker, sitting in the front seat smoking a cigarette. The outlaws' automobile was facing east when Dodson pulled it out, but as soon as the gang was ready to leave, Barrow wheeled the car around and took off, heading west.[228]

Upon learning of the shooting, lawmen hurried to the scene of the incident, where they found Campbell already dead. Investigators discovered an empty machine gun clip, a shotgun shell, and both Boyd's and Campbell's guns. The Ottawa County sheriff quickly organized a posse of fifteen men and gave chase after the killers, and lawmen from other agencies, including the U.S. Department of Justice, soon joined the pursuit. The driver of the desperadoes' vehicle was believed to be Clyde Barrow, and the woman with him was tentatively identified as Bonnie Parker. Headlines called Bonnie Clyde's "cigar-smoking companion," or simply his "moll." The other man was thought, at first, to be Raymond Hamilton, a longtime associate of Clyde Barrow, but he was actually Henry Methvin, whom Clyde had recently broken out of the Eastham Prison Farm in Huntsville, Texas.[229]

Leaving the scene of the shooting near Commerce, the Barrow gang sped west toward Chetopa, Kansas, with Boyd in the backseat beside

Clyde Barrow. *Author's collection.*

"Boodles" (i.e., Methvin) and Bonnie cradling a shotgun in the front seat beside Clyde. In addition to the gun Bonnie held in her lap, Boyd also noticed three automatic rifles, a second shotgun, and several pistols among the gang's weapons.[230]

About three miles from Commerce, the gang came upon a car occupied by A.N. Butterfield and his brother that was stranded in the middle of the

Bonnie and Clyde. *Courtesy of the FBI.*

road. Barrow and Methvin climbed out of the car, and one of them yelled at the men in the marooned vehicle, "We've just killed two men, and we're in a hurry!"[231]

If the statement was meant as a threat, neither Barrow nor Methvin carried through with it. Instead, they helped Butterfield and his brother move the stranded car out of the way, hopped back in their own automobile, and zoomed away toward Chetopa.[232]

They skirted Chetopa to the south and continued west to Bartlett, Kansas, where they stopped to buy gasoline. Meanwhile, authorities pursued the fugitives as far as Chetopa before losing track of them. A dragnet of lawmen "spread for miles around the Chetopa vicinity" looking for the bandits' vehicle but without success. One dubious report suggested that the gang's car had been spotted stuck in another mudhole at Banner School near Welch, Oklahoma.[233]

In reality, the Barrow gang had turned north at or near Bartlett, with Clyde still at the wheel, and made their way north toward Fort Scott. Barrow mainly wandered around on the backroads, not knowing for sure where he was going, and occasionally, he'd park at the side of the road to take a break. When he did come out on a good road, he would "open the machine up," and the speedometer would climb to as high as ninety miles an hour.[234]

In Fort Scott, the fugitives drove around aimlessly. They drove up and down Main Street several times and passed the police station at least once. On Friday afternoon, Methvin went into a drugstore in Fort Scott and bought a newspaper, which had headlines about the murder of Campbell earlier that morning. It was the first time the gang knew that they had killed the sixty-year-old constable. At first, Clyde said he was sorry "the old man" was killed but that he "had to do it." Later, however, he and the other gang members kept laughing about the shooting.[235]

The same afternoon, the gang's car got stuck in the mud near Fort Scott, and a group of high school students came by to try to push them out. When they were unsuccessful, Barrow told them to go on. He then flagged a truck down and made the driver pull the mired vehicle out. The gang's hostage, Police Chief Boyd, was sitting in the back seat the whole time, but the windows were so muddy that no one could see in.[236]

During their pell-mell flight from Commerce and their meanderings around Fort Scott, the gang talked freely with Chief Boyd and didn't seem a bit nervous. The murder of two highway patrolmen near Grapevine, Texas, the previous Sunday had been charged to the Barrow gang, but

Left: Bonnie Parker. *Author's collection.*

Opposite: Display of photographs of Commerce police chiefs, including Percy Boyd, on the wall at the Commerce Police Department. *Photograph taken by the author.*

Clyde vehemently denied the killing, saying that was one crime he was not guilty of.[237]

Bonnie told Boyd that the photograph that showed her smoking a cigar, which had been reprinted in newspapers across the country in recent months, was taken purely as a joke. She had borrowed the cigar from Clyde just for the photograph, and all the publicity about her smoking cigars was "bunk." She wanted Boyd to let it be known that she was not "a cigar addict."[238]

Bonnie had a pet rabbit with her, and during the gang's wild flight, she reached into the back seat several times to get a carrot to feed the animal.[239]

Around 10:00 p.m. on Friday, Barrow drove around Fort Scott looking for a car to steal but failed to find one that suited him. Shortly afterward, the gang drove southeast of town for about nine miles and let Boyd out unharmed in the wee hours of Saturday, April 7. Their parting advice was for him to "see a doctor." After enlisting help, Boyd was taken back to Fort Scott, where he was treated at a hospital for his minor injuries and released. Before leaving, he briefly recounted his misadventures with the Barrow gang. By 7:00 a.m., he was back home in Commerce, where, after a short nap, he retold the story in more detail.[240]

Boyd said the gangsters "treated [him] fine." They even gave him first-aid treatment for his scalp wound made by the rifle bullet that grazed the back of his head, and they gave him a clean shirt to replace the bloody one he'd been wearing since he was shot. Barrow also offered to give him a new suit, but it was too small. Boyd had twenty-five dollars on his person,

Percy Boyd
1933-1937

Chief Aubert Sidwell
1937-1959

but the gang was not interested in stealing it from him. "They seemed to have plenty of money," the weary police chief said. Boyd thought his and Campbell's shootout with the Barrow gang probably would not have happened if the constable hadn't fired first.[241]

Meanwhile, after letting Boyd out, the Barrow gang drove north, stole a car at Topeka, abandoned the shootout vehicle near Ottawa, Kansas, and then headed south toward Oklahoma. They were spotted by witnesses a time or two on Saturday as they crossed the Sooner State but managed to elude lawmen and made it safely into Texas.[242]

During their pursuit of the Barrow gang through Kansas, lawmen found a note west of Chetopa, where the gang's automobile had been mired in mud. It was written in a feminine hand and was thought to be the writing of Bonnie Parker. Among other things, the note said, "For the few people that have sons or daughters to go astray or be unjustly accused, I can add that the 'law' can be mistaken." The writer said she realized it would be hard to convince those who had never had unfriendly relations with authorities "how cruel the law can be." However, she wanted people to know that the B— gang had been unjustly charged over the past two years with many crimes they had not committed.[243]

On May 23, about a month and a half after the Barrow gang's murder of Cal Campbell in Commerce, Bonnie and Clyde were killed in a hail of bullets from lawmen who had laid a trap for the pair near Gibsland, Louisiana, after Methvin's father betrayed the couple to authorities.[244]

12

THE KIDNAPPING AND SLAYING OF THE MOSSER FAMILY

Carl and Thelma Mosser and their three children left their home near Atwood, Illinois, on the afternoon of Friday, December 29, 1950, headed for Albuquerque, New Mexico, to visit Carl's twin brother, Chris. In the early part of the following week, family members in Illinois received postcards from the Mossers postmarked from Claremore and Tulsa, Oklahoma. However, the Mossers still had not reached their destination in New Mexico, and relatives began to worry. Where had the family gone?[245]

Then, around noon on Wednesday, January 3, 1951, the Mossers' bullet-ridden and blood-spattered 1949 Chevy was found abandoned in a ditch on the northwest outskirts of Tulsa near Reservoir Hill. The discovery would lead to the largest manhunt in Oklahoma history, and the case would turn into one of the worst mass murders of the mid-twentieth century.[246]

A .32-caliber revolver, a bloodstained pocketknife, and bloody clothes, including a checkered dress that had been worn by three-year-old Pamela Sue Mosser, were found in the car. Five blood-flecked .32-caliber cartridges were also found embedded in the seats, and the keys were still in the ignition. Other items found in or near the vehicle included $200 worth of traveler's checks made out to the Mossers, the couple's drivers' licenses, a bloody blanket, and a strand of blonde hair, apparently from Pamela Sue.[247]

But there was no trace of the Mossers themselves. Investigators had little doubt that they were looking at a case of mass murder, but the location of the bodies and the identity of the killer remained mysteries. A search for the bodies in the immediate area around the abandoned car turned up no sign of the family.[248]

Mosser family.
Courtesy of Jim
Hounschell.

On Thursday, January 4, the search for the Mossers moved to Claremore, where it was learned the family had spent the previous Friday night and had eaten breakfast the next morning. They had not been seen since.[249]

Later on Thursday, law officers again shifted their focus, this time to the Oklahoma City area. A Texas man named L.B. Archer told investigators that he had been robbed, assaulted, and had his car stolen near Luther, Oklahoma, on Saturday by a hitchhiker he'd picked up in Texas on Friday night. Kermit Mackey, a farmer who lived in the Luther area, reported that he'd seen a man abandon Archer's car, wave down a vehicle with an Illinois license plate, and climb into the latter vehicle, which was carrying a man, a woman, and several kids. After he was taken to Tulsa, Mackey tentatively identified the bullet-ridden Chevy as the car he'd seen the hitchhiker climb into. In addition, Archer's description of the hijacker generally matched the description of a man whom a Tulsa resident had seen early Tuesday morning near the abandoned vehicle northwest of Tulsa.[250]

Based on descriptions given by the two men, authorities were looking for a white male; about twenty-five years old; five feet, seven inches tall; and weighing about 160 pounds. The suspect had sandy, curly hair; blue eyes; and thick lips. He was wearing a brown leather jacket and had a "drooping" right eye.[251]

A search of Archer's automobile turned up an even stronger lead in the case. Found in the vehicle was a sales slip for a .32-caliber revolver purchased in El Paso, Texas. It was the same type of weapon authorities believed was used in the Mosser crime, and the slip showed the gun had been purchased by W.E. Cook Jr.[252]

Officers were stumped by a discrepancy of over 3,100 miles in the odometer reading of the Mosser car when it was found abandoned northwest of Tulsa compared to when it had been serviced in Illinois the day before the Mossers left on their trip. Although the car abandoned northwest of Tulsa had not been reported to authorities until noon on Wednesday, January 4, witnesses reported they had seen it in that location at least a day or two earlier, and officers did not think the vehicle could have been driven so far in such a short period. They theorized that the odometer must have been tampered with or been defective.[253]

Authorities were on the right track on identifying the hijacker. William E. "Bill" Cook Jr. was indeed the villain who had waylaid the Mosser family. Born in Joplin, Missouri, in the late 1920s, Cook was left adrift as a small child after his mother died and his father abandoned the family. He went from one foster family to another but couldn't get along with any of them. Finally, he said he'd prefer the state reformatory to returning to any of his foster families, and his demand was granted. After he was released from the reformatory when he was about thirteen, Cook quickly got into trouble again when he held up a cab driver in Joplin. He was sent back to the reformatory but was soon transferred to a prison farm and, ultimately, to the main Missouri State Prison for being incorrigible.[254]

Cook, or "Cookie," as he was sometimes called, was released from prison in the summer of 1950. He returned briefly to Joplin but soon set out for California, telling his father he meant to "live by the gun." On Christmas Day 1950, Cook got drunk and hitchhiked from Blythe, California, to Mexico. After trying unsuccessfully to get a girl to come with him, he hitchhiked back to the United States. Near Lubbock, Texas, he abducted L.B. Archer and forced him to drive to the Oklahoma City area, where he robbed Archer, abandoned his car, and flagged down the Mossers.[255]

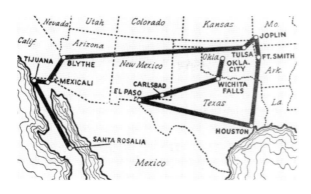

Map showing the route Cook took after kidnapping and then killing the Mossers. *From the* Carbondale Southern Illinoisian.

Although authorities were right in their identification of the suspect, they were wrong in their assumption that the Mosser car could not have been driven 3,100 miles between the time that the family left Illinois and the time that the vehicle was abandoned near Tulsa. After waylaying the Mosser family, Cook forced Carl Mosser to drive west through Oklahoma and into Texas. At Wichita Falls, Cook and Mosser went into a store, where Mosser started yelling for help, but the storekeeper thought that Mosser was just play-acting or that the two men were getting ready to rob him. Cook pulled his gun and forced Mosser back into the car. As the pell-mell journey continued west, Mosser made a similar attempt to escape or get help at Carlsbad, New Mexico, but again, Cook took control of the situation and told Mosser he'd kill him and his family if he tried anything else. The journey continued west to El Paso before Cook ordered Mosser to turn around and head back east. Mosser drove to Houston, turned north, and continued in that direction along the western edge of Arkansas and into Missouri.[256]

Cook and his captives stopped at the side of the road on the outskirts of Cook's hometown of Joplin in the wee hours of January 2, 1951. He later claimed he was getting ready to release his hostages, but when a police car came by and flashed its spotlight on the Mosser car, Mrs. Mosser and her kids started screaming and Cook started shooting. After killing all five members of the family, Cook took the wheel and drove around Joplin for an hour or so before dumping the bodies in an abandoned mine shaft in the neighborhood where he'd grown up.[257]

He then drove to Tulsa and abandoned the Mosser vehicle later that day. He got a lift into Tulsa and from there made his way to California riding buses and hitchhiking. Meanwhile, the search for the Mossers expanded from the Tulsa and Oklahoma City area to all of Oklahoma and into surrounding states.[258]

William E. "Bill" Cook II, shortly after his arrest. *Author's collection.*

On Saturday, January 6, Cook kidnapped a deputy sheriff near Blythe, California, and confessed to him that he had killed the Mossers and dumped their bodies in the snow somewhere in Oklahoma. Cook released the deputy but took his vehicle. Later the same day, Cook waylaid a motorist named Robert Dewey, killed him, and stole his car. The search for the bodies of the Mossers intensified but turned up nothing, and Cook remained on the run.[259]

On January 15, Cook was captured in Mexico and quickly brought back to the United States. Claiming blackouts, he said he had no knowledge of having killed anybody, but the same day, authorities uncovered gruesome evidence of the bloody trail he'd left. Acting on a tip from an old cellmate of Cook's, officers found the bodies of the Mossers at the bottom of an abandoned mine shaft on the west side of Joplin. The bodies were brought to the surface, laid out side by side, and photographed for newspapers. A few days later, Cook retracted his claim of blackouts and gave a full confession for the killings of not only the Mossers but Robert Dewey as well.[260]

The confessed killer was brought back to Oklahoma City to stand trial on federal charges of kidnapping and killing the Mossers. He pleaded guilty, but a sanity hearing was held on March 20 to determine whether he was mentally competent to enter such a plea. The next day, the judge abruptly ended the hearing and denied a jury trial, sentencing Cook to three hundred years in federal prison at Alcatraz.[261]

Cook was released to California authorities, however, to stand trial on state charges of murdering Robert Dewey. At his trial in November 1951 at El Centro, Cook was found guilty of first-degree murder and sentenced to death.[262]

Sullen and defiant until the end, Cook was executed in the gas chamber at San Quentin on December 12, 1952. But Oklahoma had not quite seen the last of Bill Cook. Glen Boydston, a funeral director from Comanche, was present at the execution to take charge of the body and bring it back to Oklahoma at the request of Cook family members who'd agreed to the arrangement with the understanding that Boydston would conduct a small memorial service for the deceased at Comanche before forwarding the body to Missouri for burial. The "memorial," however, turned into a circus, as thousands of curious spectators came by the funeral home to view the notorious mass murderer's body. Angry family members hurried to Comanche to remove the body to Joplin, where it was buried on the evening of December 17 in a private ceremony at Peace Church Cemetery.[263]

13

THE MURDER OF PROSECUTOR JACK BURRIS

A round 9:00 p.m. on Saturday, June 7, 1952, thirty-five-year-old Jack Burris, prosecuting attorney of Mayes County, Oklahoma, drove his small utility tractor up to an air conditioner at the side of his home near Locust Grove and left the lights shining on the appliance while he went inside the house to get some tools. When he emerged from the back door moments later, he was met by a shotgun blast that struck him in the face and killed him instantly.[264]

His wife, Melba, heard the blast and discovered Burris's body when she went to the back door to investigate. Retreating back into the house, she hysterically telephoned for help.[265]

A local physician sped to the scene, but there was nothing he could do except declare Burris dead. The victim had been struck in the neck and the lower part of his jaw, and part of the lower right side of his face had been blown away completely.[266]

H.F. Greathouse, a Locust Grove marshal, arrived around the same time as the doctor, and the county sheriff, Ralph Willcutt, reached the scene soon afterward. Greathouse, who was also a lifelong friend of Burris, thought the murder was "obviously a vengeance killing. I guess Jack prosecuted too hard somewhere. Everybody except those he sent to jail loved him."[267]

Investigators found a spent twelve-gauge shotgun shell about twelve or thirteen feet from the body near the southeast corner of the house, which was thought to be the spot from where the assassin had fired the gun. The ejector markings on the brass casing of the shell were considered an important clue that might help authorities identify the murder weapon.[268]

Jack Burris. *From the* Tulsa Daily World.

Mrs. Burris told Sheriff Willcutt that she had not seen or heard the killer aside from the shotgun blast, but she said she later heard a car driving away on a road that bordered the Burris ranch. The highway patrol was called in, and they blockaded the roads leading away from Locust Grove in every direction. Only one car that was stopped contained a shotgun, but the driver was soon allowed to go after it was established that he had nothing to do with the killing.[269]

Bloodhounds were also brought in, and they led investigators to two or three different spots behind and to the side of the Burris house, where the killer had apparently lain in wait for his victim. The dogs also traced the path the killer had taken from the Burris home through a field to the road where Mrs. Burris had heard a car drive away.[270]

At the request of Sheriff Willcutt, the Oklahoma State Crime Bureau entered the investigation, and several officers from the bureau arrived in Mayes County on Sunday, June 8. One of their first steps was to summon a locksmith to open Burris's office safe at the courthouse, under the assumption that it might contain evidence that would shed light on his murder. They found several bottles of confiscated whiskey, some papers, and a few other items but nothing that offered any definite leads.[271]

Meanwhile, the man who was appointed to temporarily replace Burris as county attorney, Bill Thomas Jr., vowed to leave no stone unturned in finding and prosecuting his predecessor's killer, and the Oklahoma governor pledged the state's full support. Sheriff Willcutt and other investigators generally shared Marshal Greathouse's opinion that the murder was a vengeance killing, and the attention of lawmen initially focused on those whom Burris had prosecuted recently.[272]

The opinion that the murder was a vengeance killing was more than mere speculation. Burris had received threats in recent months related to his actions as county prosecutor. Friends and associates said it was obvious Burris had been under some sort of strain in the days leading up to his murder. "Something was bothering him," said Sheriff Willcutt, who talked at length with Burris on the night before his killing. "He was worried about some of the threats that had been made against him."[273]

Pryor County Attorney Is Slain From Ambush At Locust Grove Home

Headline announcing the murder of Jack Burris. *From the* Oklahoma City Daily Oklahoman.

Among the early suspects wanted for questioning were Burl Houston Paddock and Harold Woodruff. Paddock, a twenty-two-year-old man who'd recently been charged with burglary, was picked up at Sapulpa on June 9 and released after questioning when authorities became convinced he had nothing to do with the murder. Woodruff, a thirty-four-year-old Jay resident, was married to a cousin of Burris's wife, and he'd been seen in Locust Grove the day before the murder arguing with Burris. He had previously been charged with obtaining property under false pretenses and released on bond. The case languished for some time, but Woodruff had jumped bail when he learned that Burris intended to press forward with the case.[274]

Several other men were also questioned, including former sheriff W.G. Robinson, who'd been known to clash with Burris when he was still in office. Their disagreements stemmed mainly, according to Robinson, from the fact that Burris did not zealously prosecute bootleggers and gamblers after Robinson arrested them. Robinson, however, was able to prove to the satisfaction of investigators that he had nothing to do with the murder of Burris.[275]

A day or so after Burris's office safe was searched, investigators revealed that a memorandum found among the papers in the safe contained the names of six liquor dealers in the Grand Lake resort region of northeastern Mayes County. In the past, liquor and gambling laws had been openly violated in the area, but Burris had apparently been trying to clamp down on the illegal activities in recent months. Under the theory that Burris's efforts to rein in the illicit gambling and liquor sales might have had something to do with his death, investigators planned to question all six of the men listed on the memorandum.[276]

On Tuesday, June 11, the *Tulsa Tribune* turned over to the state crime bureau some wire recordings Burris had given to a *Tribune* reporter several months earlier. At least one of the recordings was given to the reporter while the newspaperman was investigating crime in northeast Oklahoma, particularly in the Grand Lake area. At the time, Burris had told the reporter, "Things are happening and they might get pretty bad for me." In turning the recordings over, the *Tribune* agreed not to reveal their contents as long as the investigation into Burris's murder was ongoing.[277]

Another theory of the Burris murder that was being pursued was the possibility that the Davenport brothers' gang was involved. Norman and Chester Davenport of Wichita Falls, Texas, had been convicted in Mayes County the previous year of kidnapping and been sentenced to twenty-five years in prison, and the Oklahoma Court of Appeals had recently denied their appeal of the verdict. The Davenports had made the appeal on the basis of a claim that Burris had promised to recommend they serve only a ten-year sentence, and they had bitterly denounced the prosecutor after the appeal was denied, proclaiming that they'd been double-crossed. Authorities thought members of the brothers' gang might have exacted revenge by killing Burris, and lawmen began checking to see whether any members of the gang were in the Locust Grove area when the prosecutor was killed.[278]

On June 12, Harold Woodruff, the man who'd jumped bond when he learned Burris was going to prosecute the case against him, was cleared of any involvement in the prosecutor's death. Woodruff had left for Alaska weeks before Burris was killed and was there at the time of the murder.[279]

The elimination of Woodruff as a suspect temporarily shifted more focus to the Davenports. Authorities also questioned two of the men named in the recordings turned over by the *Tribune* the day before, but crime bureau chief George Wilson declined to discuss those interviews.[280]

Officers also began looking into Burris's movements in the days leading up to the night of his murder. It was learned that Burris's wife lived with him only on weekends, staying with her parents in Jay during the week, and Burris had reportedly been seen driving on the roads of Mayes County in the wee hours of the morning at least a time or two during the week before his murder. Witnesses had also seen people coming and going from his home at odd hours.[281]

Questioned at the state prison in McAlester, the Davenport brothers denied any knowledge of any sort of plot to kill Jack Burris, and although authorities did not immediately drop the Davenport angle of investigation, they were inclined to believe the brothers were telling the truth. On Friday, June 13, almost a week after Burris's murder, Chief Wilson announced that the investigation into the crime was at a temporary dead end. Every line of investigation pursued so far had led nowhere, he said.[282]

On Monday, June 16, however, Wilson identified two new avenues of investigation that lawmen were pursuing. Over the past few days, more than two thousand pickup trucks in a four-county area around Locust Grove had been checked out in an effort to find one that closely matched the description given by witnesses of a pickup they saw parked near the Burris home near the time of the murder. Investigators were also continuing to look into the possibility that the killing was linked to underworld crime in the Grand Lake area. At first, illegal liquor had been the main focus of that aspect of the investigation, but now, lawmen were looking more closely at the possibility that a fight over control of slot machines and other illegal, coin-operated machines in the lake area might have been a motive for the murder.[283]

Although Sheriff Willcutt claimed more than two weeks after the Burris murder that he and other lawmen were still "making headway" in the case, the reality was that the investigation was slowly losing steam. Officers had run down hundreds of leads and were continuing to check out additional ones, but all of them led nowhere.[284]

Then on the night of June 26 and in the early morning of June 27, Oklahoma Crime Bureau agents conducted a "shakedown" in northeast Oklahoma. Officers first seized a 1950 Chevrolet pickup from a car lot in Miami. The vehicle was identified as the one used as a getaway vehicle in the Burris murder. It had been under surveillance for ten days and had been traded in for a new truck earlier in the week.[285]

Immediately after seizing the pickup, officers began the operation in earnest. They raided seven businesses in the Afton area, confiscated contraband and possible evidence, and arrested a number of suspects. The confiscated items included slot machines, other gambling devices, a large quantity of whiskey, and a number of weapons, including three shotguns that authorities planned to test to see whether one might have been the gun used in the Burris slaying. Among the places raided was the Southern Mansion, operated by T.H. Bluejacket, who also ran Betty's Glass Slipper, a night spot in Afton that had been blasted to pieces with dynamite or nitroglycerin three or four nights earlier. Lawmen thought there might be some sort of connection between the explosion and the Burris killing.[286]

Bureau chief Wilson said C.E. Dawson, an Afton man known as "the kingpin slot machine operator in the Grand Lake area," was the owner of the suspected pickup at the time of Burris's murder. Dawson also owned at least one of the raided nightclubs, the Southern Mansion. Curiously enough, however, Dawson was not among the men arrested in the sting as possible suspects in the Burris murder, although he faced charges related to his gambling operations.[287]

One of the men arrested in the shakedown was held as a serious suspect and questioned at length the next day, but authorities declined to reveal his identity. Several others who were arrested were released after preliminary questioning. The prime suspect was also released a day or two later when, after he was grilled extensively, officers were unable to make a solid connection between him and the Burris killing.[288]

A day or two after the "hot" suspect was released due to a lack of evidence, the three shotguns confiscated during the Afton raid were ruled out as the Burris murder weapon, based on tests performed by ballistics experts. Investigators were left floundering for leads in the case. They were still operating under the assumption that the killing was related to gambling and other illegal activities in the Grand Lake region and that it was likely a murder for hire, but Chief Wilson admitted that they had "no real suspect in the case." Even the supposed link between the pickup seen at the scene of the crime and the one confiscated in Miami "fizzled" as a lead. In mid-July, the state crime bureau closed the temporary office it had set up in Pryor, the Mayes County seat, shortly after the murder.[289]

The *Tulsa Tribune* published multiple articles later in the year complaining about the lack of progress in the Burris case. According to the *Tribune*, the crime bureau had been on the verge of solving the case when it "suddenly dropped the angles it was pursuing." Although the articles did not mention C.E. Dawson by name, the writers wondered why the Afton slot machine kingpin whose vehicle had been linked to the murder had never been arrested. The newspaper also lamented the fact that the whiskey joints and gambling dens that had been raided in Ottawa County and eastern Mayes County had been allowed to resume operations after very brief closures.[290]

The Burris case was revived in late January 1953, when Bob Jenkins and three other men were arrested in Carthage, Missouri, in connection with a liquor store burglary. Jenkins was an escapee from the Louisiana State Prison and a former Vinita nightclub operator who had been associated with Bluejacket and Dawson when he ran the Vinita club. He was taken to Joplin, Missouri, where he was questioned for over two hours by local police and Oklahoma lawmen who rushed to the scene, but he denied any involvement in the Burris murder. Unable to establish such a connection, authorities held Dawson for extradition to Louisiana. However, he was later released on bond, and still later, he and his codefendants in the liquor store burglary case had the charges against them dropped after the owner of the liquor store mysteriously disappeared. It was reported at the time that the store's owner had been told to "get lost" until after the investigation cooled off.[291]

The controversial Burris case became even more controversial in May 1953, when Slim Weaver, the new Mayes County sheriff, accused the Oklahoma Crime Bureau of withholding information and evidence related to the case from local authorities. Weaver said the case had been "a big, dark secret that the crime bureau doesn't want to share with anybody." State officials denied that they had not cooperated with Mayes County authorities, but O.K. Bivens, George Wilson's successor as head of the crime bureau, admitted that he was not going to release the bureau's detailed report of the case because some of the information in it had been given by confidential informants. Bivens did state flatly for the first time, however, that Burris was murdered because of a conflict with "liquor and slot machine interests."[292]

The assurances from the crime bureau did not placate either Weaver or Burris's successor as Mayes County attorney, Frank Grayson. Grayson thought the bureau should turn over all its evidence to the county for study and analysis in the area where the crime occurred, especially since much of the evidence had been gathered in Mayes County. At the same time that he was complaining about lack of cooperation from the crime bureau, Grayson also announced that he and Sheriff Weaver were working on a new lead in the Burris case that he thought might help solve it. However, he declined to specify exactly what the new clue was.[293]

Nothing came of this latest lead, and the Burris case gradually went cold. In May 1956, the *Tulsa World* ran an article summarizing the case and lamenting that Burris's killer or killers would probably "never be punished." Interviewed for the article, Bivens, who was still running the crime bureau, virtually admitted that investigators knew who was responsible for Burris's murder but said they did not know the identity of the trigger man and did not have enough evidence against the conspirators who had hired him to get an indictment against them. The death of Jack Burris, the *World* concluded, "stands as a moment of triumph for crime."[294]

Just a day or two after the *Tulsa World* article appeared, Robert Hendricks, the condemned killer of a Vinita cattleman, told a pardon and parole board that he was present when bootleggers and gamblers in northeast Oklahoma plotted the murder of Burris on a farm near Spavinaw. Hendricks, who was seeking a commutation of his death sentence, said a man who'd been found dead in Adair County in January 1955 was one of the two hitmen hired by the whiskey runners and gamblers to kill Burris. According to Hendricks, the dead hitman was murdered by some of the same men who'd hired him for the Burris job. Hendricks named several of the bootleggers and whiskey runners who were present when Burris's death was plotted, but he said he did not know the names of the two hitman, just that he'd heard one of them was later killed in Adair County. Authorities confirmed that the body of a man who'd been shot and killed was found near Stilwell in January 1955. Hendricks said he rode along when Ream Payton, the man he was later convicted of killing, drove to the Spavinaw farm to lend money to some of the whiskey dealers.[295]

After the Hendricks story broke, Bivins traveled to the state prison to interrogate him. Even though he'd provided the names of some of those present at the Spavinaw farm to the parole board, Hendricks refused to divulge any details related to the Burris case to the bureau chief.[296]

On the eve his execution in early February 1957, Hendricks again asserted, this time to a *Tulsa Tribune* reporter, that he had information pertaining to the Burris murder. He said the information was contained in some letters he was writing and that he wanted the letters to be turned over to reporters after his death. Hendricks was executed on February 5, but the state prison warden at first refused to turn the letters over. A few days later, he released three of them, but the letters contained few specifics related to the Burris case and were mostly just Hendricks's rambling attempts to exonerate himself of the Payton murder.[297]

The letters did, however, spur a renewed interest in the Burris case and put pressure on the state crime bureau to release its file on the case to Mayes County authorities. After Bill Thomas, who'd served briefly as Mayes County prosecutor after Burris's death and who was now the duly elected prosecutor, received the file, he announced on February 12 that he had uncovered new avenues of investigation based on a comparison of the information in the file to the information generated locally that he was already in possession of.[298]

What exactly those new leads were Thomas declined to say, and four months later, authorities seemed no closer to solving the case. In early June 1957, the *Tulsa World* ran an anniversary feature on the case, lamenting that the murder was no closer to being solved than it had been five years earlier, right after it was committed. Another five years passed, and in June 1962, the *Tulsa World* published a ten-year anniversary story on the crime, bemoaning the fact that the crime was still not solved and probably never would be. The *World* said,

> *Ten long years have passed since an assassin's blast slew Mayes County Atty. Jack Burris. The heavy feet of time have stamped the evidence into the buttery disarray.*

Even the so-called facts are hazy now, and the first county attorney to be murdered from ambush in Oklahoma is still unavenged.

No one will say the case is closed. But the search is at an end. No one seeks Jack Burris' slayer. Musty files and newspaper clippings are all that remain.[299]

Now, over seventy years after the murder of Jack Burris, the crime is still shrouded in mystery, and it remains one of Oklahoma's most infamous unsolved crimes.

14
THE GIRL SCOUT MURDERS

Around 6:00 a.m. on Monday, June 13, 1977, Carla Wilhite, a counselor at the Camp Scott Girl Scout camp near Locust Grove, awoke and started jogging up the trail toward the main campground to take a shower. Along the way, she spotted three sleeping bags off to the side of the trail beneath a tree. What she discovered when she approached was a horrifying scene. On or near one of the sleeping bags was the body of a little girl. Her legs were spread apart, and she stared at Miss Wilhite with unseeing eyes. The other two sleeping bags were zipped closed. Thinking there had been some sort of accident, Carla ran and told another counselor of her discovery. The two notified the camp director, who, along with her husband and a camp nurse, found two more dead little girls inside the other two sleeping bags.[300]

The bodies of all three girls, ages eight, nine, and ten, had been bludgeoned, and they were nude from the waist down. Authorities were quickly summoned, and officers from the local police department, the Mayes County Sheriff's Department, the Oklahoma Highway Patrol, and the Oklahoma State Bureau of Investigation rushed to the scene.[301]

Over one hundred girls, ranging in age from second grade to high school, had arrived at Camp Scott, 1.7 miles south of Locust Grove, the day before to begin a two-week encampment, but the camp was called off and the girls sent home by bus shortly after the bodies were discovered.[302]

An initial investigation suggested that the three girls, whose names were not immediately released, had been beaten to death. At least two of their bodies also showed signs of sexual molestation. The sleeping bags that contained the bodies were located about 120 yards southeast of the platform tent to which the girls had been assigned. Two of the cots inside the tent were bloodstained, indicating that at least two of the murders had taken place there and that the killer had carried the bodies to where they were found.[303]

A large flashlight, which might have been dropped by the killer, was found near the bodies. Investigators planned to check it for fingerprints, and they also lifted fingerprints from the bodies, using a new, highly technical process.[304]

Several girls said they had heard screams around 3:00 a.m., but they did not report the sounds at the time because screams and giggles were common in the Girl Scout camp, especially during the first night. No suspects were identified in the immediate aftermath of the crime, although authorities were working from the theory that one person, a man, had committed the heinous deed. An official who was not directly involved in the investigation further revealed that lawmen had their eye on a man with a history of child molestation, but he would not name the person.[305]

Camp Scott was arranged so that several sections or units surrounded a permanent shelter that had cooking and restroom facilities. Each unit consisted of several tents perched about two feet off the ground and spaced about seventy-five feet apart. The Kiowa Unit, where the victims had been assigned, was the unit nearest to the outside boundary of the 410-acre camp, and the girls' tent was on the outside edge of the Kiowa Unit. Only one road led into Camp Scott, but another road wound to within about ¼ mile of the Kiowa Unit. Investigators theorized that the killer had entered the campground on foot and that he was familiar with the area and the layout of the camp. Evidence was found that suggested the killer may have entered the tent where the young women assigned as counselors to the Kiowa Unit were staying before he turned his attention to the little girls.[306]

The day after the murders, newspapers published the names of the three girls: eight-year-old Lori Lee Farmer of Tulsa, nine-year-old Michelle Guse of Broken Arrow, and ten-year-old Doris Denise Milner of Tulsa. Autopsies conducted by the state medical examiner's office revealed that all three girls had been beaten. Lori and Michelle had been killed by blows to the back of the head, while Doris had been sexually assaulted and strangled to death. A cord about the size of a ski rope and a towel were found wrapped around her neck, and her hands were bound behind her with adhesive tape. It was later revealed that the other two girls also showed signs of sexual molestation.[307]

LORI LEE FARMER

Lori Lee Farmer, one of the victims of the Girl Scout killer. *From the* Tulsa World.

A couple of days after the killings, three tracking dogs, including a highly trained German shepherd called the "super dog," were brought in from Pennsylvania in the hopes that they could pick up the scent of the killer and lead lawmen to him. The dogs led lawmen to a farmhouse located near the campground, where investigators found duct tape and a ski rope matching the items left at the murder scene. The farm owner, who told lawmen that his place had been burglarized around the time of the killings, was questioned but not as a suspect. He was given a lie detector test "by mutual agreement" and was released after the tests showed no signs of deception on his part.[308]

Numerous other people, including residents who lived in the area surrounding the camp, were questioned, but no solid leads were uncovered. A week after the killings, the investigation was "sputtering," as one Tulsa newspaper phrased it. The murder weapon had not been found, and there were no definite suspects. Several residents expressed their belief that the killer was still hiding out in the rugged hills surrounding the Girl Scout camp, and they thought lawmen should thoroughly comb the area, even if the National Guard had to be brought in. Others criticized investigators for not bringing in tracking dogs immediately after the murders.[309]

Perhaps in response to the criticism, investigators organized a search party a couple of days later to thoroughly scour the heavily wooded area south of Locust Grove. They also announced a partial news blackout on the case, claiming that erroneous reports by some news outlets had hampered the investigation. Regular news conferences would no longer be held. At the same time, however, lawmen released for publication two tattered pictures containing the images of three women, which had been found near the site of the murders. They asked for the public's help in identifying the women in the hope that the pictures might have been left by the killer.[310]

One day after the photographs were published, three women from southwestern Oklahoma were identified as the women in the pictures. The photographs had been taken at a wedding in the Mangum-Granite area in 1968. The women were all friends of the bride, but at least one of them said she did not know the two other women. How did such photographs turn up three hundred miles away nine years later near the site of a brutal crime? Had the killer carried them to the scene and inadvertently dropped them, or was their mysterious appearance near the Girl Scout camp completely unrelated to the murders?[311]

The answer came quickly when it was learned on June 23 that Locust Grove native Gene Leroy Hart had developed the photographs while he was incarcerated at the Granite Reformatory almost ten years earlier. Hart, a convicted rapist who'd been at large ever since his escape from the Mayes County Jail in 1973, was promptly named as the prime suspect in the murder of the three Girl Scouts. Authorities speculated that he might have been hiding out in the rugged hills surrounding the Girl Scout camp ever since his escape because he knew the countryside well and was considered a "real backwoodsman." A former local football hero, Hart had many relatives and friends in the area who could have sheltered him. A thirty-three-year-old "huskily built Cherokee Indian," Hart was described as a "seven-time loser" whose run-ins with the law dated to his youth.[312]

Later, on the same day Hart was named as a suspect, a farmer flushed a man from a cave about three or four miles southwest of Locust Grove. The farmer told lawmen he'd seen the man's leg sticking out of the cave, and when he approached, the man took off running carrying two guns. Authorities speculated that the weapons might have been a 20-gauge shotgun and a .22-caliber rifle that had been taken in a farmhouse burglary a few days earlier. Investigators found cigarettes and a sausage can inside the cave, and those items were tentatively tied to a grocery store burglary at nearby Sam's Corner a couple of days earlier. Lawmen sealed off a large area surrounding the cave and began scouring the countryside. Twice during the afternoon, searchers caught glimpses of a man running, but bloodhounds lost the man's track.[313]

The next day, June 24, the FBI was called in to help with the search. While not directly involved in the manhunt, about two hundred volunteers also scoured the area around Camp Scott for clues. The search turned up only a few meager clues, such as a footprint that authorities planned to make a plaster cast of.[314]

Two weeks after the Girl Scout killings, the man who was seen running from the cave, presumed to be Hart, had not been captured, even though authorities were convinced he was still in the area. Residents of the neighborhood remained on edge, because they, too, felt sure the suspect was still in the vicinity. Responding to accusations from family and friends of the suspect, Native activists, and other critics who said authorities were laser-focused only on Gene Leroy Hart, Mayes County district attorney Sid Wise said that, while there was evidence to suggest that Hart was the killer, law officers were still actively investigating other possibilities. Around the same time, authorities released a composite drawing of what they thought Hart looked like based on an assumption that he had slimmed down since prison mug shots had been taken of him several years earlier.[315]

Several reward funds seeking information that might lead to the arrest and conviction of Hart were set up during July. On July 25, a number of Natives met secretly with Hart, and a few days later, one of them, an activist with AIM (the American Indian Movement), told reporters that Hart claimed he was innocent but that he was afraid he would "have the hell shot out of him" if he tried to surrender. Hart said the only reason he fled officers at first was because he knew he was wanted for breaking out of jail four years earlier. The AIM member said he believed Hart's avowal of innocence.[316]

Around the same time the Natives met with Hart, some strange occurrences took place in and around Camp Scott. A pair of shoes with the name of one of the Girl Scout victims mysteriously turned up at the camp, and several sightings of a man or the silhouette of a man were reported. Based on these events, Mayes County authorities undertook another search for Hart in the area around the camp but turned up no sign of him. Afterward, Sheriff Pete Weaver said he wasn't sure the alleged meeting with Hart had even taken place and that reporters might have been "sold a bill of goods."[317]

Hart continued to elude lawmen throughout the last half of 1977 and into 1978. In late January 1978, the FBI released new sketches of Hart based on information gained from people who had seen him before or after the Girl Scout slayings. Authorities thought Hart was still in Oklahoma but not necessarily in the immediate area of the Girl Scout camp.[318]

Hart was finally captured on April 6, 1978, ten months after the murders, at a "three room shack" near Bunch, where he'd been staying with a man named Sam Pigeon Jr. Hart was arrested when six agents of the Oklahoma Crime Bureau surrounded the house. When two of them kicked in the front door, Hart tried to flee out the back door but was quickly corralled by the other agents. He was not armed and offered very little resistance. Thus ended the largest manhunt in Oklahoma history.[319]

The crime bureau revealed after the arrest that they were acting on tips they had received over the past couple of months that "a stranger" was living with an old man in the rugged Cookson Hills of east-central Oklahoma. After his arrest, Hart was taken to the crime bureau regional office in

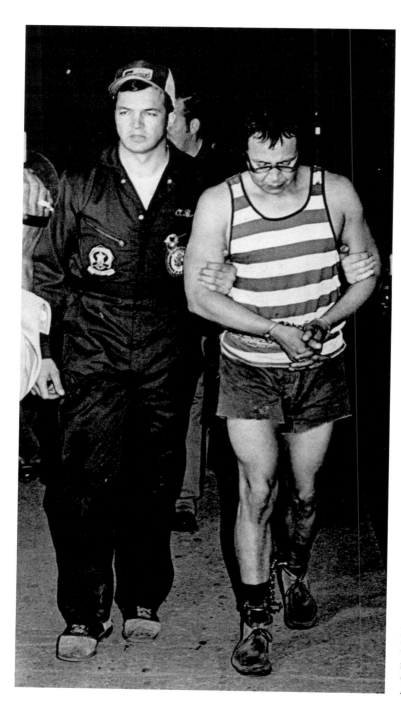

Gene Leroy Hart, escorted by a lawman, arrives at the state prison shortly after his arrest for the Girl Scout murders. *Oklahoma Historical Society.*

Tahlequah for positive identification before he was moved to the state prison at McAlester, where he was placed on death row as a security precaution. The next day, he was flown to Pryor for his arraignment and held in the Mayes County Jail.[320]

Pigeon, who was not home at the time of Hart's apprehension, was described as an elderly man who, like Hart, was a full-blooded Cherokee. He was later arrested and charged with harboring a fugitive but quickly released. Pigeon, who spoke Cherokee well but who spoke little English, told reporters that Hart had been staying with him since the previous August.[321]

In the wake of Hart's arrest, many observers said they either did not think he was guilty of the murders or did not think he could get a fair trial. How could anyone, they asked, who had been named early on as the only suspect in such a high-profile case get a fair trial? Some even compared Hart in a romantic vein to past outlaws, like Henry Starr and Pretty Boy Floyd, who'd used these same Cookson Hills as a hideout from the law.[322]

Hart pleaded not guilty to the Girl Scout murders at his first appearance in court on April 11, and his preliminary hearing was set for early June. A few days later, he was removed from the Mayes County Jail and taken to an undisclosed location for safekeeping. On April 18, Hart voluntarily gave blood, saliva, and hair samples at Grand Valley Hospital in Pryor and then was moved back to the state prison at McAlester to await his preliminary hearing.[323]

When the preliminary hearing began on June 7, over one hundred spectators packed into the Mayes County courtroom to witness the proceedings, and another two hundred watched on a closed-circuit television in a nearby auditorium. Many of the attendees were family, friends, and supporters of Hart.[324]

When the preliminary hearing finally ended a month later, the judge ruled that each of the three girls had been the victim of first-degree murder and that there was probable cause to believe Hart had committed the crimes. He was ordered to stand trial for the murders.[325]

Hart was formally arraigned in late October 1978, and after some delay, his trial got underway in Pryor in March 1979. The prosecution called an Oklahoma state chemist who testified that hair taken from the body of one of the dead girls microscopically matched hair samples taken from Hart after his arrest. Another expert witness said that sperm samples taken from Hart's underwear after his arrest were very similar to swabs taken from the bodies of the murder victim, but he could not say that they were an exact match. The prosecution relied heavily on circumstantial evidence, such as the fact that items taken from the tent of a counselor at the Girl Scout campground around the time of the murders were later found in the cabin where Hart was arrested almost fifty miles away. The defense countered that law officers, especially Sheriff Weaver, had made up their minds early on that Hart was guilty, that they never adequately investigated other possibilities, and that they might have even planted evidence against the defendant.[326]

The jury got the case on Thursday, March 29, and deliberated for four hours before recessing until the next day. On Friday morning, the jury was out for another forty minutes before they came back with a unanimous verdict of not guilty. One juror told reporters that he and his fellow jury members had actually reached an agreement after only five minutes on Thursday but had decided to deliberate further in order to "be certain" and to sleep on their decision before rendering the verdict.[327]

When the verdict was announced, the courtroom erupted into pandemonium as Hart's many family members and other supporters who were in attendance jumped up and began shouting and applauding. The prosecution team and law officers involved in the investigation, on the other hand, were shocked and dismayed by the verdict. Sheriff Weaver, for instance, said he did not intend to reopen the investigation because "we had the right man."[328]

Although he'd been acquitted of the Girl Scout murders, Hart was transported to the state prison at McAlester to resume serving his sentences totaling 145 to 305 years for rape, kidnapping, and burglary that he faced at the time of his escape from the Mayes County Jail.[329]

On June 4, 1979, barely over two months after his acquittal, Hart collapsed and died from a massive heart attack after exercising in the prison yard.[330]

Despite Hart's acquittal, most, if not all, law enforcement officials associated with the case continued to believe that he was guilty, and the case was never reopened. Years later, Sheriff Weaver said he was still haunted by the case and would never understand how people could turn "a man like Gene Leroy Hart" into a folk hero. Officially, the Girl Scout murders remain an unsolved murder, but biological tests done on evidence taken from the crime scene since the advent of DNA forensics have strongly suggested that authorities did, indeed, have "the right man."[331]

15

THE FREEMAN–BIBLE MURDER CASE

After a woman's body was found in a burning mobile home a few miles west of Welch, Oklahoma, in the early morning of December 30, 1999, initial reports made the case sound relatively unextraordinary. The December 31 *Tulsa World* reported only that a woman's body had been found among the burning rubble of forty-year-old Danny Freeman's home but that identification was being withheld pending notification of family. Investigators learned that Danny Freeman had talked to family members by phone around 8:00 p.m. the previous evening and told them his wife, Cathy, had taken their daughter Ashley and Ashley's friend Lauria Bible to a pizza parlor to celebrate Ashley's sixteenth birthday. However, all the family cars were at the mobile home, suggesting that the three must have returned before the fire. Yet no one other than the female victim was found on the premises. Authorities were still trying to determine whether the woman had died from burns, smoke inhalation, or foul play prior to the fire, but they did suspect arson.[332]

As it turned out, the Freeman-Bible case was anything but ordinary. It would soon become one of the most sensational and publicized criminal cases in Oklahoma history.

The woman whose body was found was believed to be Cathy Freeman, and one theory floated initially was that her husband, Danny, might have killed her and left with the girls. Freeman was reported to have been involved in illegal drugs, and he'd had brushes with the law before. However, law enforcement was treading lightly where the Freemans were concerned, because their son, Shane, after a brief crime spree of his own, had been killed by police less than two years earlier in what had been ruled a justifiable shooting.[333]

Lauria's parents, Jay and Lorene Bible, went to the Freeman home while authorities sifted through the smoldering rubble for bodies. When no sign of anyone other than Cathy Freeman was found, law officers cleared the scene, and the Bibles went home. However, they returned the next morning and, while conducting a search of their own, discovered the body of a man near where Cathy had been found. Although the positive identification of both bodies would take a couple of more days, Jay and Lorene knew the remains had to be those of Danny Freeman. But there was still no sign of their daughter or of Ashley Freeman.[334]

On January 2, 2000, authorities officially confirmed that the victims were Danny and Cathy Freeman, and they announced at the same time that the two had died from shotgun blasts prior to the fire. Law enforcement had suspected foul play from the beginning. Now it was official. Someone had killed the Freemans and apparently abducted the two girls.[335]

The focus turned to the missing girls. Superintendent Duane Thomas of the tiny Bluejacket School District, which Lauria attended, said everyone at the school was like family and that he and others in the Bluejacket area were praying for the return of Lauria and her friend. Students at Welch, where Ashley went to school, donned yellow ribbons and tied them up around town in support of the girls, and the First Baptist Church in Welch held a prayer vigil for them. Investigators also prioritized the search for the missing girls, but there were few actual leads in the case.[336]

During the first week after the girls' disappearance, volunteers and law enforcement officers searched the area around the Freemans' home for miles in every direction until authorities said they were running out of places to look. In addition, posters were put up on the door of almost every business in the region, and hundreds of flyers with pictures of the missing girls were handed out.[337]

At the end of the first week, investigators received a tip that led them to Picher, about twenty miles northeast of Welch, where divers began searching abandoned mines on January 5. Two days later, the search was suspended when no sign of the missing teens turned up, but a spokesman for the FBI, which had been called in on the case, said he still felt confident, based on anonymous tips, that searchers should continue to focus on the Picher area. Meanwhile, Lauria's parents waited and prayed.[338]

On January 10, a week and a half after the murders of the Freemans and the presumed abduction of the girls, the Craig County prosecutor

Search for girls moves to lake

Top: Photograph of the missing girls, Ashley Freeman (*left*) and Lauria Bible, which was distributed on posters and flyers. *From the* Oklahoma City Daily Oklahoman.

Bottom: Newspaper headline announces one of the many searches for the girls. *From the* Oklahoma City Daily Oklahoman.

announced that the investigation into the crimes was being reduced and that, without fresh leads, it was nearly at a dead end. A week or two later, a new tip prompted authorities to search Grand Lake in Delaware County in hope of finding the girls, but that search, too, proved fruitless.[339]

In late January, the case was highlighted on the TV show *America's Most Wanted*, and pictures of the girls were shown. Although the show generated several reported sightings of the girls, none of them panned out.[340]

The case was quickly turning cold, but the Bible and Freeman families refused to give up. In late January and early February, Lorene Bible spearheaded a petition drive to ask Governor Frank Keating to ensure that the investigation into the disappearance of her daughter and Ashley Freeman remained a high priority. She also helped organize a benefit in Welch that raised about $35,000 to go toward a reward for information leading to a break in the case.[341]

Some people, particularly members of the Freeman family, were suspicious of the Craig County Sheriff Department's handling of the Freeman-Bible case. In late February, two officers, including the deputy who had shot and killed Shane Freeman two years earlier, took and passed polygraph tests to try to dispel those suspicions.[342]

In early June, acting on a tip the Bibles had received, authorities searched a quarry at the north end of Oologah Lake near Chelsea, but the search, like previous ones, turned up no trace of the missing girls. By the end of 2000, the first anniversary of the crime, authorities were no closer to knowing who killed Danny and Cathy Freeman or what happened to Ashley Freeman and Lauria Bible than they had been in the early days of the investigation. The combined effort of local, state, and federal agencies; the intense regional media coverage in the immediate wake of the crime; the subsequent national attention; the thousands of flyers handed out bearing photographs of and vital statistics on the girls; and a $50,000 reward had all proved fruitless.[343]

The investigation seemed almost at a standstill, but tips kept trickling in over the ensuing months and years. Based on a tip from a jailhouse snitch, authorities searched the former home of a drug suspect near Wyandotte in late July 2001, but a bloodstained carpet found on the property showed no link to the Freeman-Bible case. In mid-May 2002, Texas death row inmate Tommy Lynn Sells wrote a letter to a Joplin, Missouri newspaper in which he claimed he had been involved in the killings of Ashley Freeman and Lauria Bible and that he knew where their bodies were buried. But authorities ultimately determined, after Sells was brought to Oklahoma, that he was lying just to get a day out of prison. Acting on a tip from a private citizen, authorities searched another property near Wyandotte in January 2003 but found nothing but horse bones in a sludge pit. In 2005, serial killer Jeremy Jones told lawmen that he had killed the girls and dumped their bodies in a mine pit near Galena, Kansas. Although Jones recanted the confession, authorities searched the Galena area over a two- or three-day period but turned up no sign of the missing girls.[344]

In 2010, Ashley Freeman was declared legally dead by her family, but that didn't mean authorities were giving up on solving the case or that the families were giving up on finding the girls. It also didn't mean that the publicity surrounding the case stopped. In 2011, the case was featured on the *Vanished with Beth Holloway* show on the Lifetime network, and an *Out of the Ashes* TV special on Investigation Discovery featured the case in 2013.[345]

After eighteen years of chasing tips that led nowhere, authorities finally got a break in the case in 2017, when Craig County sheriff Heath Winfrey found some long-overlooked notes and documents that had been stored in an office crate by a previous sheriff's administration. Following up on the discovery, authorities announced that the items had proved "extremely valuable" in generating new leads and new suspects in the Freeman-Bible case. Specific details, however, were not revealed until an arrest was made in the case the following year.[346]

At a news conference in Vinita on April 23, 2018, authorities announced that sixty-six-year-old Ronald Dean Busick had been arrested and charged for the murders of Danny and Cathy Freeman and the abduction and subsequent murders of Ashley Freeman and Lauria Bible. Two other suspects in the case, Warren Philip Welch II and David A. Pennington, had died in 2007 and 2015, respectively.[347]

Ronald Busick shortly after his 2018 arrest in the Freeman-Bible murder case. *Courtesy KSNF/KODE and fourstateshomepage.com.*

According to an affidavit released during the news conference, authorities had evidence that the three men had gone to the Freeman home around midnight on December 30, 1999, to collect a drug-related debt when the girls walked in unexpectedly. Welch was thought to be the leader of the gang and the trigger man who killed Danny and Cathy Freeman, while the other two men set fire to their trailer.[348]

The three men abducted the girls and took them to Welch's trailer home in Picher, where they tortured and raped them over a period of days before they strangled them to death and dumped their bodies in a local mine pit. During the girls' captivity, the men took Polaroid pictures of them lying on a bed bound and gagged, which Welch later showed to several people as trophies of his heinous deed. All three men had previous criminal records, with Welch's record being the most violent.[349]

It was revealed at the time of the news conference that the case could have been solved very early on if authorities had followed up on clues found by private investigators Joe Dugan and Tom Pryor. Just a day or two after the murder of the Freemans, the two investigators found an insurance verification card near the rubble of the Freemans' home. Soon afterward, Pryor located the car associated with the insurance card in a salvage yard, but when he tried to turn his findings over to authorities, he was told the car had gone through too many hands to be processed for evidence. After Sheriff Winfrey took office in 2017 and found some old notes pertaining to the insurance card, other authorities became involved, and Pryor turned the insurance card and vehicle registration over to Oklahoma State Bureau of Investigation officials. Following up on the information, authorities learned that the vehicle named on the card, a blue sedan, had belonged to Welch's former girlfriend. The car matched the description of one seen by a witness in the vicinity of the Freeman home on the night of the crime, and Welch's ex-girlfriend told authorities that Welch often drove her car around the time of the Freeman murders.[350]

After Busick's arrest was announced, the Freeman and Bible families expressed their anger and frustration over an investigation that they felt had been "grossly mishandled." Danny Freeman's stepbrother, Dwayne Vancil, who had hired the private investigators, said he was onto Welch, Pennington, and Busick as likely suspects within the first two weeks after the crime was committed but that authorities had brushed him off when he tried to put them on the trail of the three men.[351]

On April 25, two days after the news conference, Busick was brought from Wichita, where he had been arrested, to the Craig County Jail at Vinita. The next day, Lorene Bible talked to Busick through a glass window at the jail to try to learn where her daughter and Ashley had been dumped, but he told her he didn't know where their bodies were.[352]

In July 2020, in an agreement with the prosecution, Busick pleaded guilty to a reduced charge of being an accessory to murder. Terms of the deal called for Busick to serve a sentence of fifteen years, ten in the custody of the Oklahoma Department of Corrections and five under supervised release. Time already served would be subtracted from the sentence, and Busick could further reduce his sentence by another five years if he gave information that led authorities to the bodies of Lauria Bible and Ashley Freeman. Although Lorene Bible had said when Busick was first arrested that he should get the death penalty, she and other family members agreed to the plea deal in the hopes that Busick would provide information that would bring the girls home.[353]

In August, Busick did give information that led authorities to a root cellar in Picher, but a search of the location turned up no sign of the girls. At a formal sentencing on August 31, the judge, therefore, pronounced that Busick would serve his full ten-year sentence, plus five years' probation, minus time already served since his arrest.[354]

Over the next year or so, authorities searched other places based on information provided by Busick, but the new searches, like the previous ones, yielded no sign of the girls.[355]

Despite the fact that Busick's information proved worthless, he was released from prison in mid-May 2023 after serving only about half of his ten-year sentence, counting the county time he had served while awaiting trial. He still had five years of probation, but only one year of that would be officially supervised. The Department of Corrections officially said Busick had received outstanding evaluations while imprisoned, which, under state law, had earned him the early out.[356]

The Bible family and their supporters expressed outrage over Busick's early release. Lorene Bible said she never would have agreed to the plea bargain if she had been informed that Busick could be released so early.[357]

Spurred to action by Busick's early release, the Bible family spearheaded an effort that resulted in a bill called Lauria and Ashley's Law being introduced in the Oklahoma legislature in June 2023. As of this writing, the bill has passed in the House but has stalled in the Senate. If ultimately enacted into law, it would add "accessory to murder" to the list of crimes requiring convicts to serve at least 85 percent of their time before being eligible for parole. Lisa Bible Brodrick, a cousin of Lauria Bible, said after the bill was introduced that, if passed, it would bring a small measure of comfort to the Bible family to know that Lauria and Ashley's Law might alleviate the suffering of other families, even a little.[358]

Meanwhile, the quest to locate the girls' bodies and bring them home for proper burial goes on. New searches are undertaken as new leads come to light. Anyone with information that might be relevant to the girls' whereabouts can contact authorities or the Bible family through a Facebook page titled "Find Lauria Bible-BBI."

NOTES

Chapter 1

1. Ross, "Murder of Boudinot," 19.
2. Hicks, "Cherokees vs. Jackson."
3. Ibid.
4. Ibid.; Docs Teach, "Analyzing the Petition."
5. Hicks, "Cherokees vs. Jackson."
6. Docs Teach, "Analyzing the Petition."
7. Ibid.; Ross, "Murder of Boudinot," 20; Pate, "Major Ridge."
8. Ross, "Murder of Boudinot," 20–21; "History of the Cherokee Feud," *Macon* (MS) *Intelligencer*, October 10, 1839.
9. "Cherokee Feud," *Macon* (MS) *Intelligencer*; Ross, "Murder of Boudinot," 23.
10. "Death of Ridge," *St. Louis Niles National Register*, August 3, 1839; "Cherokee Feud," *Macon* (MS) *Intelligencer*.
11. "Death of Ridge," *St. Louis Niles National Register*.
12. Ibid.
13. Ibid.
14. Ross, "Murder of Boudinot," 21.
15. "Cherokee Feud," *Macon* (MS) *Intelligencer*; *Richmond* (VA) *Enquirer*, August 9, 1839; Ross, "Murder of Boudinot," 25–26.
16. "Death of Ridge," *St. Louis Niles National Register*; "Cherokee Feud," *Macon* (MS) *Intelligencer*.
17. Christ, "Stand Watie."

Chapter 2

18. "The Going-Snake Butchery," *Chicago Tribune*, April 22, 1872 (quoting the *Fort Smith New Era*); "The Going-Snake Butchery: Another Side," *Chicago Tribune*, April 29, 1872 (quoting the *Tahlequah Cherokee Advocate*).

19. "Going-Snake Butchery," *Chicago Tribune*; Weiser-Alexander, "Goingsnake Massacre."

20. Weiser-Alexander, "Goingsnake Massacre"; Chance, "Tragedy at Goingsnake."

21. *Chicago Tribune*, April 22, 1872; Chance, "Tragedy at Goingsnake"; Agnew, "Tragedy," 93.

22. Agnew, "Tragedy," 93–94.

23. "Going-Snake Butchery," *Chicago Tribune*; "Butchery: Another Side," *Chicago Tribune*.

24. Agnew, "Tragedy," 95.

25. "Going-Snake Butchery," *Chicago Tribune*.

26. Ibid.

27. Ibid.

28. Ibid.

29. Ibid.

30. "Butchery: Another Side," *Chicago Tribune* (quoting the *Cherokee Advocate*).

31. Ibid.

Chapter 3

32. "A Close Call," *Tahlequah Telephone*, October 3, 1889.

33. Mihesuah, "Nede Wade 'Ned' Christie," 260–62; *Vinita Weekly Chieftain*, November 19, 1885.

34. Mihesuah, "Nede Wade 'Ned' Christie," 263–64.

35. *Eufaula* (OK) *Indian Journal*, June 4, 1885; Mihesuah, "Nede Wade 'Ned' Christie," 264.

36. "The Murder at Tahlequah," *Vinita Indian Chieftain*, May 12, 1887.

37. Mihesuah, "Nede Wade 'Ned' Christie," 266–68; "Fort Smith," *Fort Worth Daily Gazette*, November 20, 1887; "The Territory's Needs," *Fort Worth Daily Gazette*, December 21, 1887.

38. "Uncle Sam Defied," *St. Louis Globe-Democrat*, December 23, 1887.

39. "Tore His Head Off," *St. Louis Post-Dispatch*, February 24, 1888.

40. *Tahlequah Cherokee Advocate*, March 1, 1888.

41. "Close Call," *Tahlequah Telephone*; Mihesuah, "Nede Wade 'Ned' Christie," 269–70; "Noted Desperadoes," *Fort Worth Daily Gazette*, November 8, 1890.

42. Mihesuah, "Nede Wade 'Ned' Christie," 270–71; "Close Call," *Tahlequah Telephone*.

43. "Noted Desperadoes," *Fort Worth Daily Gazette*; Mihesuah, "Nede Wade 'Ned' Christie," 271.

44. "Noted Desperadoes," *Fort Worth Daily Gazette*; "That Visit to Christy," *Vinita Weekly Chieftain*, November 27, 1890.
45. "Visit to Christy," *Vinita Weekly Chieftain*; "Bass Reeves Killed," *Memphis Appeal Avalanche*, January 27, 1891; "Muskogee, I.T., Jan. 26," *Atoka* (OK) *Indian Citizen*, January 31, 1891.
46. "Officers Fight with Desperadoes," *St. Louis Globe-Democrat*, June 4, 1891.
47. "Territory Items," *Minco* (OK) *Minstrel*, July 10, 1891 (quoting the *Tahlequah Cherokee Advocate*).
48. "After Outlaws," *Guthrie Oklahoma State Capital*, October 15, 1892; "A Bandit Trapped," *Norman Transcript*, October 14, 1892.
49. "Bandit Trapped," *Norman Transcript*; "The Ned Christie Fray," *Tahlequah Cherokee Advocate*, October 12, 1892; "After Outlaws," *Guthrie Oklahoma State Capital*.
50. "Christie Fray," *Cherokee Advocate*; "Ned Christie Escapes," *Guthrie Oklahoma State Capital*, October 22, 1892.
51. "Christie Escapes," *Guthrie Oklahoma State Capital*; Mihesuah, "Nede Wade 'Ned' Christie," 272.
52. "Ned Christie Killed," *Tahlequah Cherokee Advocate*, November 9, 1892; Mihesuah, "Nede Wade 'Ned' Christie," 273.
53. Mihesuah, "Nede Wade 'Ned' Christie," 273–74; "Christie Killed," *Tahlequah Cherokee Advocate*.
54. "Ned Christie," *Guthrie Oklahoma State Capital*, November 12, 1892; "Christie Killed," *Tahlequah Cherokee Advocate*; Mihesuah, "Nede Wade 'Ned' Christie," 274–76.
55. Mihesuah, "Nede Wade 'Ned' Christie," 275–83.

Chapter 4

56. "Bob Rogers Shot," *Coffeyville* (KS) *Daily Journal*, March 16, 1895.
57. Weiser-Alexander, "Rogers Brothers."
58. "A Shocking Murder," *Vinita Weekly Chieftain*, November 10, 1892.
59. Ibid.
60. Ibid.
61. "Chelsea Station Robbed," *Vinita Weekly Chieftain*, July 6, 1893; Weiser-Alexander, "Rogers Brothers."
62. "Robbed at Noon," *Kiowa* (KS) *News-Review*, July 19, 1893; Weiser-Alexander, "Rogers Brothers."
63. "Two Outlaws Disposed Of," *Vinita Weekly Chieftain*, August 3, 1893; Weiser-Alexander, "Rogers Brothers."
64. "City and Country," *Caney* (KS) *Phoenix*, October 27, 1893.
65. "Robbers at Work," *Wichita Beacon*, December 26, 1893; Weiser-Alexander, "Rogers Brothers."
66. "Robbers at Work," *Wichita Beacon*; Weiser-Alexander, "Rogers Brothers."
67. "Robbers at Work," *Wichita Beacon*.

68. "Got One of Them," *Coffeyville Weekly Journal*, January 12, 1894.
69. "Dead or Alive," *Coffeyville Weekly Journal*, February 2, 1894; *Chickasaw* (OK) *Chieftain*, January 18, 1894; Weiser-Alexander, "Rogers Brothers."
70. "Caught Napping," *Topeka Daily Capital*, January 24, 1894; "Dead or Alive," *Coffeyville Weekly Journal*.
71. "Cracked Kernals," *Coffeyville Weekly Journal*, March 30, 1894; *Vinita Weekly Chieftain*, April 5, 1894.
72. *Coffeyville Daily Journal*, October 8, 1894; *Coffeyville Daily Journal*, March 4, 1895.
73. *Coffeyville Daily Journal*, March 4, 1895; "Hold-Up at Angola," *Coffeyville Daily Journal*, March 5, 1895; "Robbers Headed North," *Coffeyville Daily Journal*, March 6, 1895.
74. "Rogers Shot," *Coffeyville* (KS) *Daily Journal*.
75. Ibid.
76. Ibid.
77. Ibid.
78. Ibid.

Chapter 5

79. Starr, *Thrilling Events*, 9, 12; May, "Starr, Henry."
80. Starr, *Thrilling Events*, 14–22.
81. *Vinita Indian Chieftain*, December 15, 1892; Weiser-Alexander, "Henry Starr."
82. *Coffeyville Weekly Journal*, November 18, 1892; *Vinita Indian Chieftain*, December 15, 1892
83. *Vinita Indian Chieftain*, December 15, 1892; "Desperado's Deed," *Minco Minstrel*, December 23, 1892; "Henry Starr Guilty," *Tahlequah Arrow*, September 21, 1895.
84. "Desperado's Deed," *Minco Minstrel*; "Starr Guilty," *Tahlequah Arrow*.
85. "Desperado's Deed," *Minco Minstrel*; "Starr Guilty," *Tahlequah Arrow*.
86. "Desperado's Deed," *Minco Minstrel*.
87. Ibid.; *Vinita Indian Chieftain*, December 15, 1892.
88. *Purcell* (OK) *Register*, December 22, 1892; "Two Desperadoes Killed," *Pittsburg* (KS) *Daily Headlight*, January 20, 1893.
89. Starr, *Thrilling Events*, 35–36; Weiser-Alexander, "Henry Starr."
90. "Oklahoma Matters," *Norman* (OK) *Transcript*, May 12, 1893; "Train Robbery," *Vinita Weekly Chieftain*, May 4, 1893; "Bolder Than the Dalton Gang," *St. Louis Globe-Democrat*, May 4, 1893.
91. Weiser-Alexander, "Henry Starr"; "A Bold Robbery," *Russellville* (AR) *Democrat*, June 8, 1893.
92. "Starr Surprised," *Oklahoma City Oklahoma Press Gazette*, July 5, 1893.
93. Ibid.
94. "On Trial for His Life," *Green Forest* (AR) *Tribune*, October 19, 1893; Starr, *Thrilling Events*, 52.
95. "All Over the State," *Little Rock Arkansas Democrat*, January 17, 1898; Weiser-Alexander, "Henry Starr."

96. "Old Time Bank Raid," *Sayre* (OK) *Standard*, March 19, 1908; Weiser-Alexander, "Henry Starr."
97. "Got His Man," *Lamar* (CO) *Register*, May 19, 1909; "Paroled," *Lamar* (CO) *Register*, October 1, 1913; Weiser-Alexander, "Henry Starr."
98. Weiser-Alexander, "Henry Starr."
99. "Starr Admits His Guilt; 25 Years," *Tulsa Oklahoma Weekly World*, August 5, 1915; "A Parole to Henry Starr," *Chickasha Daily Express*, March 18, 1919.
100. May, "Starr, Henry."

Chapter 6

101. Burton, "Goldsby, Crawford"; Galonska, "Outlaw Trail."
102. Burton, "Goldsby, Crawford"; Galonska, "Outlaw Trail."
103. "Murder at Fort Gibson," *Muskogee Phoenix*, November 2, 1893; Galonska, "Outlaw Trail."
104. Galonska, "Outlaw Trail"; "Local Paragraphs," *Muskogee Phoenix*, July 12, 1894.
105. "News Summary," *Muskogee Our Brothers in Red*, July 26, 1894; "Desperadoes at Red Forks," *Guthrie Daily Leader*, July 20, 1894.
106. "Bank Robbery," *Chandler News-Publicist*, August 3, 1894.
107. "Robbed Parkinson at Okmulgee," *Muskogee Phoenix*, September 19, 1894.
108. "Fort Smith Letter," *Muskogee Phoenix*, September 19, 1894; Galonska, "Outlaw Trail."
109. "Valley Depot Robbed," *Claremore Progress*, October 13, 1894.
110. "The Bandit's Romance," *Oklahoma City Daily Oklahoman*, October 26, 1894.
111. "Bandit's Romance," *Oklahoma City Daily Oklahoman*; "A Chance to Make Money," *Oklahoma City State Capital*, October 29, 1894.
112. "Jim Cook on Trial," *Duncan* (OK) *Banner*, November 3, 1894.
113. "Particulars of the Robbery at Lenapah," *Coffeyville Daily Journal*, November 10, 1894; "On Trial for His Life," *Little Rock Daily Arkansas Gazette*, February 26, 1895.
114. *Coffeyville Daily Journal*, November 13, 1894.
115. "Took a Shot at Cherokee Bill," *Coffeyville Weekly Journal*, November 23, 1894.
116. "Talk with Cherokee Bill," *Eufaula Indian Journal*, November 23, 1894.
117. "The Second Time," *Coffeyville Daily Journal*, December 24, 1894.
118. "Another Time," *Coffeyville Daily Journal*, January 1, 1895.
119. Ibid.; "The Nowata Hold-Up," *Muskogee Phoenix*, January 5, 1895.
120. "Bill Cook," *Santa Fe New Mexican*, January 14, 1895; "Cherokee Bill," *Coffeyville Daily Journal*, January 30, 1895; "Cherokee Bill in Jail," *Little Rock Daily Arkansas Gazette*, January 31, 1895.
121. *Norman Peoples' Voice*, February 16, 1895; "Cherokee Bill Again Convicted," *Little Rock Daily Arkansas Gazette*, February 22, 1895; "On Trial for His Life," *Little Rock Daily Arkansas Gazette*; "Last of the Outlaws," *Little Rock Daily Arkansas Gazette*, March 1, 1895; *Muskogee Phoenix*, April 20, 1895.

122. "Killed by Cherokee Bill," *Monticello* (AR) *Monitcellonian*, August 2, 1895; Galonska, "Escape Attempt."
123. Galonska, "Escape Attempt"; "Died as He Lived," *Little Rock Daily Arkansas Gazette*, March 18, 1896.

Chapter 7

124. Crowe and Lewis, "1921 Tulsa Race Massacre"; "Arrest of Young Negro on Statutory Charge Caused Battle Between the Races," *Tulsa World*, June 1, 1921.
125. Crowe and Lewis, "1921 Tulsa Race Massacre"; "Arrest of Young Negro," *Tulsa World*.
126. "Martial Law Halts Race War," *Tulsa Tribune*, June 1, 1921; *Encyclopaedia Britannica*, "Tulsa Race Massacre of 1921."
127. "New Battle Now in Progress," *Tulsa World*, June 1, 1921.
128. Richardson, "Tulsa Race Massacre."
129. Krehbiel, "Tulsa Race Massacre"; Ellsworth, "Tulsa Race Massacre"; Oklahoma Historical Society, "Tulsa Race Riot."
130. Oklahoma Historical Society, "Tulsa Race Riot."
131. Ibid.
132. Ellsworth, "Tulsa Race Massacre"; Oklahoma Historical Society, "Tulsa Race Riot"; *Encyclopaedia Britannica*, "Tulsa Race Massacre of 1921."
133. Oklahoma Historical Society, "Tulsa Race Riot"; "Two Whites Dead in Race Riot," *Tulsa World*, June 1, 1921.
134. Oklahoma Historical Society, "Tulsa Race Riot."
135. Ibid.
136. Ibid.; "Two Whites Dead," *Tulsa World*.
137. Oklahoma Historical Society, "Tulsa Race Riot"; "Two Whites Dead," *Tulsa World*.
138. Oklahoma Historical Society, "Tulsa Race Riot"; "Two Whites Dead," *Tulsa World*; Ellsworth, "Tulsa Race Massacre."
139. Oklahoma Historical Society, "Tulsa Race Riot."
140. Ibid.
141. Ibid.
142. Ibid.
143. Ibid.
144. Ibid.
145. Ibid.
146. "Martial Law," *Tulsa Tribune*.
147. Richardson, "Tulsa Race Massacre"; Oklahoma Historical Society, "Tulsa Race Riot."
148. *Encyclopaedia Britannica*, "Tulsa Race Massacre of 1921."
149. Richardson, "Tulsa Race Massacre"; Ellsworth, "Tulsa Race Massacre."

150. *Encyclopaedia Britannica*, "Tulsa Race Massacre of 1921"; Ellsworth, "Tulsa Race Massacre."

151. *Encyclopaedia Britannica*, "Tulsa Race Massacre of 1921."

Chapter 8

152. "Indian Wife of Ponca Man Is Found," *Ponca City News*, May 28, 1921; "Find Bodies of Two Murder Victims," *Pawhuska Journal-Capital*, May 28, 1921; "Osage Woman Killed for Money, Is Claim," *Oklahoma City Daily Oklahoman*, May 30, 1921; Grann, *Killers of the Flower Moon*, 5.

153. National Archives, "Dawes Act"; Kesler, Aronczyk, Romer and Rubin, "Blood, Oil, and the Osage Nation."

154. Kesler, Aronczyk, Romer and Rubin, "Blood, Oil, and the Osage Nation."

155. Ibid.

156. Ibid.

157. Osage Nation Lessons, "Reign of Terror"; Kesler, Aronczyk, Romer and Rubin, "Blood, Oil, and the Osage Nation."

158. May, "Osage Murders"; Osage Nation, "Did You Know?"; Klein, "FBI's First Big Case."

159. "Indian Wife," *Ponca City News*; "Find Bodies of Two Murder Victims," *Pawhuska Journal-Capital*, May 30, 1921; McDonnell, "Historical People Depicted in *Killers of the Flower Moon*."

160. FBI, "*Inside the FBI* Podcast"; "Get into Arresting Habit," *Tulsa World*, August 30,1921; "Anna Brown Coroner's Jury Discharged," *Fairfax* (OK) *Osage Chief*, September 30, 1921.

161. *Fairfax Osage Chief*, July 22, 1921; May, "Osage Murders"; Linder, "Osage 'Reign of Terror.'"

162. *Fairfax Osage Chief*, February 9, 1923; Grann, *Killers of the Flower Moon*, 83–84.

163. "Two Killed in Explosion," *Hominy* (OK) *News-Republican*, March 16, 1923; "Smith Dies, Three Held," *Ponca City News*, March 17, 1923; FBI, "*Inside the FBI* Podcast."

164. "Fairfax Aroused by Blowup that Killed 2 Persons," *Tulsa World*, March 12, 1923; "Third Victim of Blast at Fairfax Dies," *Pawhuska Osage Journal*, March 15, 1923; "Two Killed," *Hominy* (OK) *News-Republican*.

165. "Former County Attorney Killed," *Anadarko* (OK) *Tribune*, July 5, 1923; Fixico, *Invasion of Indian Country*, 42; Grann, *Killers of the Flower Moon*, 93.

166. May, "Osage Murders"; Klein, "FBI's First Big Case."

167. FBI, "*Inside the FBI* Podcast"; Grann, *Killers of the Flower Moon*, 113, 190.

168. May, "Osage Murders"; Osage Nation, "Did You Know?"; Solly, "Real History."

169. Solly, "Real History."

170. "Hale and Burkhart Arrested Charged with Killing Bill Smith Here in 1923," *Fairfax Osage Chief*, January 8, 1926; "Convict Accused of Osage Murder," *Miami News-Record*, May 14, 1926; *Ada Evening News*, June 2, 1926.

171. May, "Osage Murders."

172. Ibid.

173. Ibid.; Osage Nation, "Did You Know?"

Chapter 9

174. "Detain Wike and Seeley Partners of Two Smiths Murdered in Oklahoma," *Hartford* (CT) *Courant*, April 28, 1930; "Frontier Code Is Revived for Wike and Seeley," *Hartford* (CT) *Courant*, April 30, 1930; "Severs Murders Charged to Pair," *Muskogee Daily Phoenix*, April 29, 1930; "Identify Ring in Killing," *Muskogee Times-Democrat*, April 29, 1930; "Murder Preliminary Underway," *Muskogee Times-Democrat*, May 1, 1930.

175. "Identify Ring," *Muskogee Times-Democrat*.

176. "Murder Preliminary Underway," *Muskogee Times-Democrat*.

177. "Severs Double Murder Mystery Grows Deeper," *Muskogee Daily Phoenix*, April 28, 1930.

178. Ibid.; "Severs Murders Charged," *Muskogee Daily Phoenix*.

179. "Severs Double Murder Mystery," *Muskogee Daily Phoenix*.

180. Ibid.

181. Ibid.

182. Ibid.; *Muskogee Daily Phoenix*, April 27, 1930.

183. "Severs Double Murder Mystery," *Muskogee Daily Phoenix*.

184. "Find No Logical Answer to Main Killing Theories," *Muskogee Times-Democrat*, April 28, 1930.

185. "See Vengeance in Hotel Murders," *Muskogee Times-Democrat*, April 28, 1930; "Severs Murders Charged," *Muskogee Daily Phoenix*.

186. "See Vengeance," *Muskogee Times-Democrat*.

187. Ibid.

188. Ibid.; "Severs Double Murder Mystery," *Muskogee Daily Phoenix*.

189. "Severs Murders Charged," *Muskogee Daily Phoenix*; *Muskogee Times-Democrat*, April 30, 1930.

190. "Severs Murders Charged," *Muskogee Daily Phoenix*.

191. "Seeley and Wike into Court Tomorrow," *Muskogee Times-Democrat*, April 30, 1930.

192. "Murder Preliminary Underway," *Muskogee Times-Democrat*; *Muskogee Daily Phoenix*, May 2, 1930.

193. "Preliminary Hearing for Wike-Seeley Today," *Muskogee Daily Phoenix*, May 1, 1930; "Wike and Seeley Freed of Charges," *Muskogee Daily Phoenix*, May 2, 1930; "Wike and Seeley Leave for Home Post $2000 Bond," *Muskogee Daily Phoenix*, May 3, 1930; "Papers Belonging to Smith Found on Street," *Muskogee Daily Phoenix*, May 9, 1930; "Finding of Missing Hotel Key Adds New Mystery Element to Slayings," *Muskogee Times-Democrat*, May 22, 1930.

194. "Robberies Laid to Alleged Kidnaper," *Joplin Globe*, June 5, 1930; "Fail to Identify Suspect in Murders," *Muskogee Times-Democrat*, June 17, 1930; "R.L. Benton, Murder Suspect Escapes Jail," *Muskogee Daily Phoenix*, August 3, 1930.

195. "Famed DeVol Gang Eluding Cops of West," *Muskogee Times-Democrat*, December 2, 1930; "Karpis Gangster Flees in Insane Asylum Break," *Muskogee Daily Phoenix*, June 8, 1936; "Slaying of Oklahoma City Bandit Leads to Hunt for Crazed Gunman in Famous Muskogee Murder Case," *Muskogee Daily Phoenix*, "Muskogee Slayer, Devol, Dies at Enid of Police Bullets," June 28, 1936; *Muskogee Daily Phoenix*, July 10, 1936.
196. Wikipedia, "Lawrence Devol"; Wood, *Midnight Assassinations*, 172–73.

Chapter 10

197. Noel Houston, "Guard Called Out in Floyd Hunt," *Oklahoma City Oklahoma News*, February 18, 1934.
198. Ibid.
199. Wallis, "Charles Arthur Floyd"; "Two Arrested in Oklahoma for Kroger Holdup," *St. Louis Globe-Democrat*, September 16, 1925.
200. Wallis, "Charles Arthur Floyd."
201. "Posses Hunt 'Pretty Boy' Floyd," *Bartlesville Examiner-Enterprise*, April 9, 1932; U.S. Census, 1930.
202. "Pretty Boy Floyd Kills Officer," *Muskogee Times-Democrat*, April 9, 1932.
203. Ibid.
204. "Pretty Boy Robs Bank in Home Town," *Oklahoma City News*, November 1, 1932; "Bank Held Up at Sallisaw; Floyd Blamed," *Miami News-Record*, November 1, 1932.
205. "Pretty Boy Robs Bank," *Oklahoma City News*.
206. Ibid.
207. Wallis, "Charles Arthur Floyd."
208. Houston, "Guard Called Out," *Oklahoma City News*.
209. Ibid.
210. Ibid.
211. Ibid.
212. Ibid.
213. Ibid.
214. Noel Houston, "Writer Calls Cookson Hills Fortress Which Army of 1000 Can't Capture," *Oklahoma City News*, February 19, 1934.
215. Ibid.
216. Ibid.
217. Ibid.
218. Ibid.
219. Ibid.
220. Ibid.
221. Wallis, "Charles Arthur Floyd."

Chapter 11

222. "Constable Slain, Police Chief Kidnaped by Machine Gunner Trio Near Commerce," *Miami News-Record*, April 6, 1934; "Hunt for Barrow Spreads Over Southwest," *Miami News-Record*, April 8, 1934.
223. "Hunt for Barrow Spreads," *Miami News-Record*.
224. Ibid.
225. Ibid.
226. Ibid.
227. Ibid.; "Constable Slain, Police Chief Kidnaped," *Miami News-Record*.
228. "Hunt for Barrow Spreads," *Miami News-Record*.
229. Ibid.; "Constable Slain, Police Chief Kidnaped," *Miami News-Record*; Wikipedia, "Henry Methvin."
230. "Hunt for Barrow Spreads," *Miami News-Record*.
231. Ibid.; "Constable Slain, Police Chief Kidnaped," *Miami News-Record*.
232. "Constable Slain, Police Chief Kidnaped," *Miami News-Record*.
233. Ibid.; "Hunt for Barrow Spreads," *Miami News-Record*.
234. "Hunt for Barrow Spreads," *Miami News-Record*.
235. Ibid.
236. Ibid.
237. Ibid.
238. Ibid.
239. *Tulsa World*, April 8, 1934.
240. "Barrow Frees Officer, with U.S. on Trial after Killing," *Tulsa World*, April 7, 1934; "Hunt for Barrow Spreads," *Miami News-Record*.
241. "Hunt for Barrow Spreads," *Miami News-Record*.
242. Ibid.; "Search for Barrow Given New Impetus by Finding of His Cap Near Ottawa, Kas.," *Miami News-Record*, April 9, 1934.
243. "Barrow Frees Officer," *Tulsa World*.
244. FBI History, "Bonnie and Clyde"; Wikipedia, "Bonnie and Clyde."

Chapter 12

245. "Atwood Family of Five Missing in Oklahoma; Mass Murder Feared," *Decatur* (IL) *Daily Review*, January 4, 1951; "Summary of Known Facts in Mystery," *Tulsa Tribune*, January 4, 1951.
246. "Officers Fear Family Slain in Tulsa Area," *Tulsa World*, January 4, 1951.
247. Ibid.; "Atwood Family of 5 Missing; Find Blood-Stained Car," *Decatur Herald*, January 4, 1951; "Atwood Family of Five Missing," *Decatur* (IL) *Daily Review*.
248. "Officers Fear Family Slain," *Tulsa World*.
249. "Hunt Widens for Missing Five, Slayer," *Tulsa World*, January 5, 1951.
250. Ibid.
251. Ibid.
252. Ibid.

253. Ibid.

254. "Mossers Shot to Death," *Joplin Globe*, January 16, 1951; "Case History of a Badman," *St. Louis Post-Dispatch*, January 21, 1951.

255. "Mossers Shot," *Joplin Globe*; "Case History," *St. Louis Post-Dispatch*.

256. "Mossers Shot," *Joplin Globe*; *Joplin Globe*, January 20, 1951.

257. "Mossers Shot," *Joplin Globe*; *Joplin Globe*, January 20, 1951.

258. "Escaped Kidnaper Hunted as Murderer of Five Illinoisians," *Tulsa Tribune*, January 5, 1951; "Mossers Shot," *Joplin Globe*.

259. "Ex-Convict Sought in Mosser Mystery Kidnaps California Deputy," *Tulsa World*, January 7, 1951.

260. "Mossers Shot," *Joplin Globe*; "Cook Confesses He Killed Mosser Family in Joplin," *Joplin Globe*, January 20, 1951.

261. "Doctors Disagree on Cook's Sanity," *Oklahoma City Daily Oklahoman*, March 21, 1951; "Killer Cook to Face Court in California," *Tulsa World*, March 22, 1951.

262. "Billy Cook's Execution Date Set for Dec. 12," *Salinas Californian*, October 11, 1952.

263. "Mosser Family Slayer, Bill Cook, Is Executed," *Tulsa Tribune*, December 12, 1952; "Cook Refuses to See Chaplain," *Enid Daily Eagle*, December 12, 1952; "'Roman Holiday' Ended with Burial of Billy Cook Body," *Lawton* (OK) *Morning Press*, December 18, 1952.

Chapter 13

264. "Mayes County Attorney Slain by Shotgun Blast," *Tulsa World*, June 8, 1952; "Pryor County Attorney Is Slain from Ambush at Locust Grove Home," *Oklahoma City Daily Oklahoman*, June 8, 1952.

265. "Seek Burris's Slayer," *Pryor* (OK) *Jeffersonian*, June 12, 1952.

266. Ibid.

267. "Pryor County Attorney Is Slain," *Oklahoma City Oklahoman*.

268. "Seek Burris's Slayer," *Pryor* (OK) *Jeffersonian*.

269. Ibid.

270. Ibid.

271. Ibid.

272. Ibid.

273. Ibid.

274. Ibid.; "Delaware Suspect Hunted in Burris Murder Probe," *Tulsa Tribune*, June 9, 1952.

275. "Delaware Suspect Hunted," *Tulsa Tribune*.

276. Ibid.

277. "*Tribune* Gives Burris Recordings to Agents," *Tulsa Tribune*, June 11, 1952.

278. Ibid.; "Burris Death Tie to Kidnap Case Studied," *Tulsa World*, June 12, 1952.

279. "Suspect Cleared in Burris Death," *Tulsa Tribune*, June 12, 1952.

280. Ibid.

281. Ibid.

282. "Mayes Killing Still Baffles Investigators," *Tulsa World*, June 14, 1952.

283. "Mystery Truck Gives New Lead in Killer Hunt," *Tulsa Tribune*, June 16, 1952.

284. "Manhunt for Burris's Slayer Retains Momentum in Third Week," *Pryor Jeffersonian*, June 26, 1952.

285. "Burris Slaying Suspects Jailed in Secret Spots," *Tulsa Tribune*, June 27, 1952; *Tulsa World*, June 28, 1952.

286. "Burris Slaying Suspects Jailed," *Tulsa Tribune*.

287. Ibid.; "New Lead Reported on Burris Slaying," *Tulsa World*, June 28, 1952.

288. "Burris Slaying Probers Center on One Suspect," *Tulsa Tribune*, June 28, 1952; "Burris Slaying Solution Fades," *Tulsa Tribune*, June 30, 1952.

289. "New Murder Clues Sought," *Tulsa World*, July 1, 1952; "Burris Death Clues Fizzle," *Tulsa World*, July 2, 1952; "Burris Probed Still Stymied," *Tulsa World*, July 8, 1952; "Burris Probe Hits Impasse," *Tulsa Tribune*, July 19, 1952.

290. "Four-Month-Old Burris Slaying Probe Goes On," *Tulsa Tribune*, October 7, 1952; "Burris Slaying Action Pledged," *Tulsa Tribune*, December 6, 1952.

291. "Arrest of Four Revives Burris Slaying Probe," *Tulsa Tribune*, January 22, 1953; "Robbed Liquor Dealer Missing," *Tulsa Tribune*, January 23, 1953; "Officers Quiz Ex-Vinitan in Burris Case," *Tulsa World*, January 23, 1953; "Bail Granted in Theft Case," *Tulsa World*, January 25, 1953; "4 in Robbery Case Cleared," *Tulsa World*, February 10, 1953.

292. "State to Keep Burris Slaying Report Secret," *Tulsa Tribune*, May 13, 1953.

293. "Officers Check New Lead in Year-Old Burris Slaying," *Tulsa World*, June 7, 1953.

294. "Ambush Slayers of Mayes County Aide May Never Be Punished for 1952 Crime," *Tulsa World*, May 20, 1956.

295. "Bootleggers and Gamblers Plotted Murder of Burris, Slayer Tells Parole Board," *Tulsa World*, May 23, 1956; "Burris Ambush Killer Slain, Hendricks Tells Parole Board," *Tulsa Tribune*, May 23, 1956.

296. "Burris Death Data Withheld," *Tulsa Tribune*, May 24, 1956.

297. "'Clear My Name' Killer Pleads," *Tulsa Tribune*, February 4, 1957; "Gary Promises Letter Release; Fight Snowballs," *Tulsa Tribune*, February 7, 1957; "Burris Probe Turns Up 'Important New Leads,'" *Tulsa Tribune*, February 12, 1957; "Gary Releases Three Letters by Hendricks," *Tulsa World*, February 8, 1957; "Burris Probe Is Reopened," *Tulsa World*, February 9, 1957.

298. "Probe Turns Up 'Important New Leads,'" *Tulsa Tribune*, February 12, 1957.

299. "5-Year-Old Slaying of Jack Burris Still Is Unsolved Mystery," *Tulsa World*, June 2, 1957; "Search at End for Prosecutor's Slayer," *Tulsa World*, June 2, 1962.

Chapter 14

300. "Possibility of Lesbian Killer Studied First," *Tulsa World*, June 8, 1978.

301. "3 Girl Scouts Slain at Camp," *Sapulpa* (OK) *Daily Herald*, June 13, 1977; "Three Tulsa-Area Girls Slain; Child Molester Sought," *Tulsa World*, June 14, 1977; *Tulsa World*, June 16, 1977.

302. "Three Tulsa-Area Girls Slain," *Tulsa World*; "3 Girl Scouts Slain," *Sapulpa* (OK) *Daily Herald*.

303. "Three Tulsa-Area Girls Slain," *Tulsa World*; "3 Girl Scouts Slain," *Sapulpa* (OK) *Daily Herald*.

304. "Officials Tight-Lipped on Girl Scouts' Killer," *Tulsa World*, June 15, 1977.

305. "3 Girl Scouts Slain," *Sapulpa* (OK) *Daily Herald*; "Three Tulsa-Area Girls Slain," *Tulsa World*.

306. "Three Tulsa-Area Girls Slain," *Tulsa World*; "Clues Reported Found in Scout Camp Slayings," *Tulsa World*, June 16, 1977.

307. "Three Tulsa-Area Girls Slain," *Tulsa World*.

308. "Dog Handler Vows Break in Slayings," *Tulsa World*, June 17, 1977; "Owner of Ranch Passes Lie Test," *Tulsa World*, June 18, 1977.

309. "Probe Sputtering, Signs Indicate," *Tulsa World*, June 20, 1977.

310. "Girls' Murder Probe Takes Unusual Twists," *Tulsa World*, June 22, 1977.

311. "Location of Photos Puzzles 2 Subjects," *Tulsa World*, June 23, 1977.

312. "Escapee Hunted in 3 Slayings," *Tulsa World*, June 24, 1977.

313. Ibid.; "250-Man Posse Seeking Suspect in Triple Slaying," *Lawton Constitution*, June 24, 1977.

314. "FBI Called into Search for Suspect," *Tulsa World*, June 25, 1977.

315. "Accused Murderer of 3 Scouts Still Eludes Searchers," *Tulsa World*, June 26, 1977; "Search for Murder Suspect Stalls; Officers Confident," *Tulsa World*, June 27, 1977; "Dragnet Fails to Yield Hart," *Tulsa World*, June 28, 1977; "Search for Fugitive Gene Hart Called Off," *Tulsa World*, June 29, 1977.

316. "2 Florida Men Want Girls' Killer Caught," *Tulsa World*, July 14, 1977; "Deadline Extended for Reward Fund," *Tulsa World*, July 23, 1977; "Folks in Florida Town Care About 3 Slain Scouts," *Tulsa World*, July 29, 1977; "Hart Denies Killing Girls, Fears He'll Be Shot Down," *Tulsa World*, July 30, 1977.

317. "Sheriff Not Sure Recent Reports on Hart Are Correct," *Tulsa World*, August 1, 1977.

318. "FBI Releases New Drawings of Hart," *Tulsa World*, January 31, 1978.

319. "Suspect in Slaying of Girl Scouts Captured at Cookson Hills House," *Tulsa World*, April 7, 1978; "Long Hunt Ends—Numb Grief Remains," *Tulsa World*, April 9, 1978.

320. "Suspect in Slaying of Girl Scouts Captured," *Tulsa World*; "'Quiet Man' Admits Harboring Hart," *Tulsa World*, April 8, 1978.

321. "Suspect in Slaying of Girl Scouts Captured," *Tulsa World*; "'Quiet Man' Admits," *Tulsa World*.

322. "Suspect in Slaying of Girl Scouts Captured," *Tulsa World*; "Long Hunt Ends," *Tulsa World*; "Readers Doubt Hart's Guilt," *Tulsa World*, April 16, 1978.

323. "Court Hears Hart Plead Not Guilty," *Tulsa World*, April 12, 1978; *Tulsa World*, April 17, 1978; *Tulsa World*, April 19, 1978.

324. *Tulsa World*, June 8, 1978.

325. "Suspect in Slaying of Girl Scouts Captured," *Tulsa World*.

326. "Hart Wins Round in Trial Procedure," *Tulsa World*, October 31, 1978; "Chemist Says Hairs Found Match Hart's," *Tulsa World*, March 22, 1979; "Sperm Samples Like Hart's, Biochemist Says," *Tulsa World*, March 24, 1979; "Prosecution Rests Case in Hart Trial," *Tulsa World*, March 25, 1979; "Defense Says Weaver Wanted Hart Dead," *Tulsa World*, March 27, 1979; "Hart Jury Retires to Sleep, to Resume Deliberations Today," *Tulsa World*, March 30, 1979.
327. "Hart Innocent, Case Won't Be Reopened," *Tulsa World*, March 31, 1979.
328. Ibid.; "Despite Acquittal, Hart Prison-Bound," *Oklahoma City Daily Oklahoman*, March 31, 1979.
329. "Hart Innocent," *Tulsa World*.
330. "Gene Hart Collapses, Dies," *Tulsa World*, June 5, 1979.
331. "Camp Scott Girl Scout Murders," *Tulsa World*, June 17, 2017.

Chapter 15

332. "Body Is Found in Trailer Fire," *Tulsa World*, December 31, 1999.
333. Withrow, "Welch Girls"; "Schools, Towns Pray for Two Missing Teens," *Oklahoma City Daily Oklahoman*, January 4, 2000.
334. Withrow, "Welch Girls."
335. "Schools, Towns Pray," *Oklahoma City Daily Oklahoman*.
336. Ibid.
337. "Community Lends Support After Girls' Disappearance," *Oklahoma City Daily Oklahoman*, January 8, 2000.
338. "Crews Search Sewer Ditches for Girls," *Sapulpa Daily Herald*, January 7, 2000; "Crews End Search of Mine Shafts for Missing Girls with No Clues," *Sapulpa Daily Herald*, January 9, 2000; "Hunt Goes on for Two Girls," *Oklahoma City Daily Oklahoman*, January 7, 2000.
339. "Search for Two Missing Girls Scaled Back," *Oklahoma City Daily Oklahoman*, January 11, 2000; "Search for Girls Moves to Lake," *Oklahoma City Daily Oklahoman*, January 24, 2000.
340. "Missing Girls Focus of Show," *Tulsa World*, January 21, 2000.
341. "Search for Girls Moves," *Oklahoma City Daily Oklahoman*; "Hope Endures in Welch for Two Missing Girls," *Oklahoma City Daily Oklahoman*, February 14, 2000; "Reward Increased to $40,000," *Oklahoma City Daily Oklahoman*, February 22, 2000."
342. "2 Officers Take Polygraph Tests," *Oklahoma City Daily Oklahoman*, February 24, 2000.
343. "Police Divers Fail to Find Two Girls," *Tulsa World*, June 8, 2000; "A Year Passes Without Answers," *Tulsa World*, December 30, 2000.
344. "Dog Search Reveals Nothing in Hunt for Missing Welch Girls," *Tulsa World*, June 15, 2001; "Search for Bodies Fruitless," *Tulsa World*, June 30, 2005; "Cold Case No More," *Tulsa World*, April 24, 2018; "Killer Claims to Know Welch Girls' Burial Site," *Oklahoma City Daily Oklahoman*, May 15, 2002; "Tip Prompts Search for Two Missing Girls," *Oklahoma City Daily Oklahoman*, January 25, 2003.

345. "Cold Case No More," *Tulsa World*.
346. "Found Welch Case Notes 'Extremely Valuable,'" *Tulsa World*, December 30, 2017.
347. "Cold Case No More," *Tulsa World*.
348. Ibid.
349. Ibid.; "Suspects Have Long Criminal Histories," *Tulsa World*, April 24, 2018; "Charges Filed in 1999 Killings," *Oklahoma City Daily Oklahoman*, April 24, 2018.
350. "Cold Case No More," *Tulsa World*.
351. "Old Case Called 'Grossly Mishandled,'" *Tulsa World*, April 25, 2018.
352. *Tulsa World*, April 26, 2018; *Tulsa World*, April 27, 2018.
353. "Man Pleads Guilty in Case of Missing Welch Girls," *Oklahoma City Daily Oklahoman*, July 16, 2020.
354. "'He's an Evil Man': Busick Sentenced," *Tulsa World*, September 1, 2020.
355. "Family Skeptical on Suspect's Tips," *Tulsa World*, October 7, 2020; "Search for Welch Girls Turns Up No Remains," *Tulsa World*, April 28, 2021; "Search in Picher to Resume," *Tulsa World*, October 8, 2021.
356. "Man Convicted in Welch Case Released from Prison," *Tulsa World*, May 20, 2023.
357. Ibid.
358. "New Bill Inspired by Welch Girls' Murder Case," *Tulsa World*, June 7, 2023; "Criminal Justice Reform Cited as Senate Declines 'Welch Girls' Bill," *Tulsa World*, April 26, 2024.

SELECTED BIBLIOGRAPHY

Agnew, Kelly. "Tragedy of the Goingsnake District." *Chronicles of Oklahoma* 64, no. 3 (Fall 1986): 93–94.

Burton, Art. T. "Goldsby, Crawford (1876–1896)." *Encyclopedia of Oklahoma History and Culture.* https://www.okhistory.org/publications/enc/entry. php?entry=GO006.

Chance, Will. "'Tragedy at Goingsnake' Occurred 149 Years Ago." *Tahlequah Cherokee Phoenix*, April 15, 2021.

Christ, Mark K. "Stand Watie (1806–1871)." *Encyclopedia of Arkansas.* https:// encyclopediaofarkansas.net/entries/stand-watie-14563.

Crowe, Kweku Larry, and Thabiti Lewis. "The 1921 Tulsa Race Massacre: What Happened to Black Wall Street?" *Humanities* 42, no. 1 (Winter 2021): n.p. https://www.neh.gov/article/1921-tulsa-massacre.

Docs Teach. "Analyzing the Petition Against the Treaty of New Echota." National Archives. https://www.docsteach.org/activities/teacher/analyzing-the-petition-against-the-treaty-of-new-chota#:~:text=While%20John%20Ross%20was%20 in,what%20is%20today%20eastern%20Oklahoma.

Ellsworth, Scott. "Tulsa Race Massacre." *Encyclopedia of Oklahoma History and Culture.* https://www.okhistory.org/publications/enc/entry. php?entry=TU013#:~:text=During%20the%20course%20of%20eighteen. from%20fifty%20to%20three%20hundred.

Encyclopaedia Britannica. "Tulsa Race Massacre of 1921." https://www.britannica. com/event/Tulsa-race-massacre-of-1921.

FBI. "Bonnie and Clyde." https://www.fbi.gov/history/famous-cases/bonnie-and-clyde#:~:text=Background,seen%20up%20to%20that%20time.

———. *"Inside the FBI* Podcast: The Osage Murders." https://www.fbi.gov/video-repository/inside-the-fbi-the-osage-murders-video-101923.mp4/view.

Fixico, Donald. *The Invasion of Indian Country in the Twentieth Century: American Capitalism and American Tribal Resources.* 2nd ed. Boulder: University Press of Colorado, 2012.

Galonska, Juliet. "Cherokee Bill: On the Outlaw Trail." National Park Service. https://www.nps.gov/fosm/learn/historyculture/cherokee-bill-outlaw-trail.htm.

———. "Cherokee Bill's Escape Attempt from Jail." Fort Smith National Historic Site. https://home.nps.gov/fosm/learn/historyculture/cherokee-bill-escape-attempt-from-jail.htm.

Grann, David. *Killers of the Flower Moon: The Osage Murders and the Birth of the FBI.* New York: Doubleday, 2017.

Hicks, Brian. "The Cherokees vs. Andrew Jackson." *Smithsonian Magazine*, March 2011. https://www.smithsonianmag.com/history/the-cherokees-vs-andrew-jackson-277394/.

Kesler, Sam Yellowstone, Amanda Aronczyk, Keith Romer and Willa Rubin. "Blood, Oil, and the Osage Nation: The Battle over Headrights." NPR. https://www.npr.org/2023/03/23/1165619070/osage-headrights-killers-of-the-flower-moon-fletcher-lawsuit.

Klein, Christopher. "The FBI's First Big Case: The Osage Murders." History Channel. https://www.history.com/news/the-fbis-first-big-case-the-osage-murders.

Krehbiel, Randy. "Tulsa Race Massacre: Key Figures in 1921." *Tulsa World*, May 31, 2020.

Linder, Douglas O. "The Osage 'Reign of Terror' Murder Trials: An Account." UMKC School of Law. Famous Trials. https://www.famous-trials.com/osage-home/2378-the-osage-reign-of-terror-murder-trials-an-account).

May, Jon D. "Osage Murders." *Encyclopedia of Oklahoma History and Culture.* https://www.okhistory.org/publications/enc/entry.php?entry=OS005.

———. "Starr, Henry (1873–1921)." *Encyclopedia of Oklahoma History and Culture.* https://www.okhistory.org/publications/enc/entry?entry=ST060.

McDonnell, Brandy. "Take a Look at the Historical People Depicted in *Killers of the Flower Moon*." *Oklahoma City Oklahoman*, October 23, 2023.

Mihesuah, Daniel A. "Nede Wade 'Ned' Christie and the Outlaw Mystique." *Chronicles of Oklahoma* (Fall 2015): 260–89.

National Archives. "Dawes Act (1887)." https://www.archives.gov/milestone-documents/dawes-act.

Oklahoma Historical Society. "Tulsa Race Riot: A Report by the Oklahoma Commission to Study the Tulsa Race Riot of 1921." https://www.okhistory.org/research/forms/freport.pdf.

Osage Nation. "Did You Know? Osage Murders, the Reign of Terror." https://www.osagenation-nsn.gov/news-events/news/did-you-know-osage-murders.

Osage Nation Lessons. "Reign of Terror: The Osage Indian Murders Fact Sheet." https://osagenation.s3.amazonaws.com/G/G.1.a.ReignTerrorFactSheet.pdf.

Pate, James P. "Major Ridge." *Encyclopedia of Oklahoma History and Culture.* https://www.okhistory.org/publications/enc/entry?entry=RI005.

Richardson, Randi. "Tulsa Race Massacre, 100 Years Later: Why It Happened and Why It's Still Relevant Today." NBC News. https://www.nbcnews.com/news/nbcblk/tulsa-race-massacre-100-years-later-why-n1268877.

Ross, Allen. "The Murder of Elias Boudinot." *Chronicles of Oklahoma* 12, no.1 (March 1934): 19–24.

Solly, Meilan. "The Real History Behind *Killers of the Flower Moon*." *Smithsonian*, October 18, 2023. https://www.smithsonianmag.com/history/the-real-history-behind-killers-of-the-flower-moon-180983086/.

Starr, Henry. *Thrilling Events: Life of Henry Starr*. Originally printed, 1914. College Station, TX: Creative Publishing Company, 1982.

U.S. Census. www.familysearch.org.

Wallis, Michael. "Charles Arthur Floyd 1904–1934." *Encyclopedia of Oklahoma History and Culture*. https://www.okhistory.org/publications/enc/entry.php?entry=FL004.

Weiser-Alexander, Kathy. "The Goingsnake Massacre or the Cherokee Courtroom Shootout." Legends of America. https://www.legendsofamerica.com/cherokee-courtroom-shoot-out.

———. "Henry Starr the Cherokee Bad Boy." Legends of America. https://www.legendsofamerica.com/we-henrystarr.

———. "Rogers Brothers Gang of Outlaws." Legends of America. https://www.legendsofamerica.com/rogers-brothers-gang.

Wikipedia. "Bonnie and Clyde." https://en.wikipedia.org/wiki/Bonnie_and_Clyde.

———. "Henry Methvin." https://en.wikipedia.org/wiki/Henry_Methvin.

———. "Lawrence Devol." https://en.wikipedia.org/wiki/Lawrence_DeVol.

Withrow, Brooke. "The Welch Girls: A Look Inside the Decades-Old Cold Case." KOCO News 5, Oklahoma City. https://www.koco.com/article/oklahoma-welch-girls-cold-case-picher-ashley-freeman-lauria-bible/41759447.

Wood, Larry E. *Midnight Assassinations and Other Evildoings: A Criminal History of Jasper County, Mo*. Joplin, MO: Hickory Press, 2020.

INDEX

G

Galena, Kansas 114
Gibsland, Louisiana 87
Goingsnake District 16, 22
Goldsby, Crawford (alias Cherokee Bill)
 42, 43, 44, 45, 46, 47, 48
Grand Lake 96, 97, 98, 99, 113
Grayhorse, Oklahoma 59, 61
Grayson, Frank 100
Greathouse, H.F. 94, 95
Greenwood District 49, 50, 51, 58
Grinnett, Bear 23
Guse, Michelle 104

H

Hale, William K. "Bill" 61, 63, 64
Halleck, Ralph 30
Hamilton, Raymond 82
Hardgrave, Ben 76
Harrison, Arkansas 41
Hart, Gene Leroy 106, 107, 109, 110
Hendricks, Robert 100, 101
Hildebrand Mill 14, 16
Houston, Noel 78, 79, 80
Houston, Texas 91

I

Illinois River 78
Isbell, L.P. 23

J

Jackson, Andrew 9, 11
James, Frank 44
James, Jesse 44
Jay, Oklahoma 96, 97
Jenkins, Bob 99
Jones, Jeremy 114
Jones, Lee 66, 68
Joplin, Missouri 39, 40, 81, 90, 91,
 93, 99

K

Kansas City Massacre 77
Kansas City, Missouri 75
Karpis, Alvin 74
Keating, Frank 114
Keating, Larry 48
Keetoowah Society 15
Kelley, Erv 76
Kelly, George "Machine Gun" 75
Kesterson, J.L. 14, 16
Killers of the Flower Moon 65
Kirksville, Missouri 74
Ku Klux Klan 50
Kyle, Lizzie Q. 61
Kyle, Minnie 60, 61

L

Lenapah, Oklahoma 36, 45, 48
Lewis, Jake 42
Locust Grove, Oklahoma 94, 95, 96,
 97, 98, 103, 105, 106
Lott, M.M. 43
Lubbock, Texas 90

M

Mackey, Kermit 89
Maples, Daniel 22, 23, 28
Mason, B.F. 59
Mayes County, Oklahoma 38, 95, 96,
 97, 99, 100
McAlester, Oklahoma 40, 78, 97,
 109, 110
McCullough, W.M. 50
Melton, Ernest 45, 48
Methvin, Henry 82, 83, 85, 87
Miami, Oklahoma 73, 98, 99
Milner, Doris Denise 104
Morrison, Kelsie 64
Mosser, Carl 88, 91
Mosser, Chris 88
Mosser, Pamela Sue 88
Mosser, Thelma 88, 91
Mound Valley Bank 30

ABOUT THE AUTHOR

L arry Wood is a retired public schoolteacher and a freelance writer specializing in the history of the Ozarks and surrounding regions. He is the author of twenty-five books, including nine previous titles published by The History Press. His articles and short stories have appeared in numerous national and regional publications, ranging from *Wild West* magazine to the *Missouri Historical Review*. Wood maintains a blog on regional history at www.ozarks-history.blogspot.com.